COSMIC LOVE
AND HUMAN WRONG

COSMIC LOVE
AND HUMAN WRONG

The Reconception of the Meaning of Sin,
in the Light of Process Thinking

by
William **Norman Pittenger**

PAULIST PRESS
New York/Ramsey/Toronto

Acknowledgement
F.W. Dillstone, *The Christian Faith*.
London, Hodder and Stoughton, 1964.
Used with permission.

Library of Congress
Catalog Card Number: 77-99301

ISBN: 0-8091-2093-3

Published by Paulist Press
Editorial Office: 1865 Broadway, New York, N.Y. 10023
Business Office: 545 Island Road, Ramsey, N.J. 07446

Printed and bound in the
United States of America

Contents

For
Bill and Rosemary Hurdman
in gratitude for
a deep friendship
and many kindnesses

Preface

The chapters in this book were originally delivered as lectures at Texas Christian University, Fort Worth, Texas, in 1971. Since that time, the material (either as it now stands or in part) has been given in lectures at other American and British universities and theological schools and also before British Christian theological groups, both Catholic and Protestant, during the past four years. I am grateful to the many people who have asked me to speak, to the audiences who kindly listened to what I had to say, and for the comments and criticisms that have led me to make numerous changes in the text. I have retained the conversational tone of the original lectures, however, and have not attempted completely to rewrite the material, since I believe that the informal mode of presentation may make the position I advocate more readily intelligible to those who are not professional theologians.

The point of the book is sufficiently indicated by the title. I am urging that we greatly need a reconception of sin, perhaps even with the abandonment, for the time being, of the word itself. This should not suggest that I am minimizing the appalling reality of the fact to which the word points: Human life *is* estranged from its intended destiny and *is* alienated from God and fellow humans by wilful acts whose consequences are truly horrific. But the conventional idiom seems to me often to fail to convey this reality to many of our contemporaries. And in the effort to make the truth of the matter understandable to modern people who, like all human beings, are sinners, I have used the conceptuality called "Process Thought", since I believe that this is both more satisfactory for our own day than any other and is also able to provide a genuine continuity with the traditional theology of the Catholic Church, even when it departs from

1

some of the commonly accepted ideas found in that theology.

The reader will notice that from time to time I have made use of the insights of depth psychology, but I have not given that kind of psychology the attention it may well merit. The reasons for this are two: First, I am not expert in the field and I think it inadvisable for an amateur to venture into it; and second, several books have already been published that explore the contributions of that kind of psychological analysis to the concept of sin. The late Paul Tillich, for one, did this in many articles and on many occasions; so also have the late David Roberts and the still happily living Albert Outler, to mention but two of the many who might be named. I believe that what is said in these chapters, particularly in the third and fifth, is in general agreement with the views of those who have been able to speak with authority on the psychological aspects of the subject.

Let me conclude by saying that I am much indebted, in my own thinking, to Dr. Bernard Lee of St. Louis, who has done valiant service to the cause of reconceiving Catholic theology in process terms, and also to several of my colleagues in the divinity faculty of this university, both Catholic and Protestant, with whom I have been privileged to discuss the subject. I am responsible, of course, for everything said first in the lectures and now in the book that includes them.

King's College   Norman Pittenger
University of Cambridge
England

1
Rethinking the Concept of Sin

The purpose of this book is to engage with my readers in a rethinking of the concept of sin. My suggestion will be that this concept, as it has been traditionally presented, no longer makes much sense to men and women in their concrete contemporary existence. If this is true, as I am sure it is, what we need today is some other way of describing the appalling fact in human experience to which that concept points. Notice that I am not saying that it is impossible to talk any longer about sin and about sins. I am saying that the traditional way of doing so does not serve us. The reasons for my thinking this may be stated briefly.

As the word "sin" is commonly understood by the people with whom we talk today, it either has no meaning at all, save as a piece of religious jargon, or it is almost entirely misunderstood in respect to its basic significance. What do I intend by saying this? Before I attempt to answer that question in more detail, I wish to point out that the general title of this book does not imply that we should give up the word altogether, no matter what some people may take it to suggest. Neither does my title suggest any denial of the reality in experience to which the word "sin" and the traditional concept of sin have pointed. I believe that we must find some other way of describing this reality and perhaps in that fashion do something to restore the word to its proper usage. That enterprise will engage us throughout this study.

Now I realize very well that in spite of this precise indication of my purpose some will assume that I am rejecting as incredible and outworn not only the use of the word in its mistaken interpretation or the concept as we have inherited it but also the recognition of the fact of sin. There are always

3

plenty of people who simply will not understand, perhaps will not wish to understand, the difference between a term or a concept, a phrase or a word, and whatever it my be that such a term, concept, phrase, or word has been used to indicate. And in no area of human experience is this inability or refusal more frequently found than in religious discourse or theological discussion.

For some reason many theologians and many good pious people do not understand this simple distinction. Sometimes, indeed, it would seem that they are so enamoured of the words they use, words that have for them a certain sacred character because they have been in currency for a long time, that they *identify* them with the things the words were first intended to describe. The difference between an abiding reality in human experience and the phraseology that for many people and over many years has conveyed its meaning would appear to be fairly obvious, yet often the difference is not grasped. But surely words are not so important as that which they denote.

Some words have acquired what Paul Tillich used to call "power"—they are so much part of the inherited human tradition and so evocative of depths of meaning that it is difficult to see how they can be given up. Tillich felt that a word like "grace" was an example; this word, he believed, has enormous "power" even today. Yet we must also confess that when words have become nearly meaningless to the minds of most of our contemporaries, the insistence that they must unfailingly be used seems a little absurd. What is true of words is equally, if not more patently, true of concepts. Insistence upon their retention smacks of idolatry—it is confusing reality with terminology.

In our own day the great word "God" has fallen victim to this loss of meaning for a considerable number of our contemporaries. "God" has been so much identified with various ideas that are radically false that one group of modern Christian thinkers proposes to us that we no longer use it. Such writers and thinkers have sought to find terms that in their judgment will be more communicative of meaning in the present situation; some few of them have even ventured to think that the word, and the concept that goes with it, can no longer serve at all—we must have a "godless" Christianity. To me this last suggestion borders on sheer nonsense, if anything like authentic Christian faith is in view. As to the former proposal, I confess that I am of two minds. I recognize perfectly well the mistaken ideas that the word "God" suggests to many today; one of my major concerns in recent years has been to urge the association of that word with cosmic loving persuasion or sheer goodness, participant in the world and human experience, rather than with notions of un-moved mover, impassive substance, moral ruthlessness, and the like. At the same time I think that the word "God" is still useful and valuable, especially since there is no other readily available single word to use for the purpose. My feeling is that we should continue to use the word "God", but that when we use it today we follow it with some phrase like "that is to say" or "in other words", thus giving it the content that we believe is correct and that can be made meaningful to our hearers.

I am not at all sure that the word "sin" is in this same category. So far as I can see, its significance has been so much misunderstood or perverted that we are desperately in need of some other way of conveying what we are talking about. I do not have any particular substitute to offer. Nor do I propose any single new notion to replace the traditional concept of sin. I *do* believe that the kind of approach I shall advocate will be of help to many in thinking through the problem; and I think that some of the various terms I shall myself employ in this interpretation may succeed in conveying a meaning to those who, so soon as they hear the word "sin" or listen to talk about the traditional concept associated with that word, immediately begin to entertain all the *wrong* ideas—or just turn off their receiving-apparatus and pay no attention at all.

Probably it is silly to labour the obvious, but I wonder if my readers have had my own experience when they have had occasion in public discussion to use the word "sin" or to discuss the conventional theological concept of sin. I have discovered that very often, once I have started, nobody is attending to what is being said. It is all a matter of "in-talk" for theologians or religious-minded people; outside the "circle of religion" it means nothing, has nothing to do with ordinary life. So far as some auditors are concerned, one might just as well be talking in an entirely unknown tongue.

What is perhaps worse, the word has suggested ideas that have been remote from my own mind. Most frequently, the word "sin" appears to suggest something about sexual misbehaviour; so much so, indeed, that "sin" and "sex" are thought by many to be nearly synonymous in Christian talk. "They were living in sin" was the phrase used by an older generation to describe a man and woman who lived together without having gone through the ceremony of marriage. Another notion has been that sin means simply and solely the breaking of a commandment or set of rules, or an act of disobedience to a precisely stated moral code set up by God himself and arbitrarily imposed upon the human race. Thus when somebody "breaks" a commandment or disobeys a prescription in the conventional moral code, he is guilty of sin. A legalistic conception of the meaning of sin is thought to be part of the Christian way of seeing things. But surely none of us would wish to accept any such interpretation.

It is true that one way in which the reality intended by the concept of sin manifests itself is in the sphere of sexual life; it is also true that there is a sense in which the breaking of a moral law, however understood, can be taken as part of the meaning of human sinning. But no informed and thoughtful Christian, surely no responsible theologian, assumes that these constitute the deepest significance of the genuine fact the word and concept were devised to indicate. That fact is both more serious than the common understanding and also less readily restricted to such specific behaviour. In recent times we have been told over and over again—and rightly—that sin is a specifically *religious* concept. That is to say, it has to do with the relationship between God and humankind; and here the stress comes on the word "relationship." Even when the places where we sin have no immediate and obvious reference to divine and human meeting, this remains the case. Most often, both in the teaching of the Old Testament prophets and in the words of Jesus, the places and the occasions for sin are indeed human and "secular"; yet precisely because God is inescapably present in such human and secular places and his purpose or will is to be done in them, there is always a reference to him in whatever people may do, whether for good or for evil. Sin *is* religious in connotation, not simply a matter of the moral law.

Such considerations have persuaded me that we may need to soft-pedal the *word* "sin", at least for the present. Perhaps one day, when mistaken ideas and wrong associations have been forgotten, the word can come back in all its original power; and we may hope that it will do so. Why do I say this? The answer is simply that the word, or its equivalents in other languages than English, is so much a part of the biblical literature, so much a term in the heritage of Christian thought, that we cannot wish to throw it away. It ought to be able to regain its power. There have been times when it has suggested the right things—which in this case of course were the "wrong things", so far as authentic human existence is concerned—and when its use has been profoundly meaningful. This is obvious in Holy Scripture; and since the Bible is so central a part, indeed the normative part, of the Christian tradition, we want very much to be able to use its language without embarrassment, so far as this is possible for us. Yet even here we must beware of confusing the thing of which the Bible speaks with the biblical word. In a sense quite different from that historically meant by "nominalism", we are always in danger of falling victim to what we may style "the nominalistic fallacy."

Why not treat "sin" as we have suggested we should treat the word "God"? That is, continue to use the term, but after every use of it add some phrase that will make the meaning clear. I agree with this proposal, so far as we can find a word or words that will serve the purpose, and in this book I shall often follow this procedure. At the same time I should urge that we try also to find *other* ways of speaking, especially when we are engaged in explanation of basic Christian convictions to those who are ill-informed or antagonistic or who for one reason or another find that they are inhibited from understanding our meaning when we use the conventional idiom. Perhaps this whole set of terms is "too far gone" to be used regularly today, even in Christian worship; it may be that we shall be wise to

rephrase parts of that worship, especially in the public confes-
sion of sin that forms part of normal Christian services of
worship, so that what we are talking about will emerge crystal-
clear.

In any event, our present concern is with rethinking or
reinterpreting. That is the important matter, and it is my belief
that certain contemporary movements of thought will help us in
doing this job. Much of our time, therefore, will be given to
those aspects of existentialism and process thinking that I take
to be useful for our purpose. But first I must make another
preliminary remark.

We should honestly admit that a great deal of Christian talk
has been sin-obsessed. Historically this certainly has been the
case, and even today there are those who so much stress the
sinfulness of human existence that they make the whole Christian enterprise revolve around it. Yet surely the very heart of the
gospel is not about our sin but rather is about God's gracious
love. On one occasion I said in a lecture, using scriptural language, "The Christian message is much less centered in 'the old
Adam in whom we die' than in 'the new Adam in whom we are
made alive.' " It has been a mistake to focus attention on the
negative rather than the positive side of the gospel proclamation. And that mistake has been responsible for the idea, so
strange to those familiar with the New Testament emphasis, that
the Christian faith is primarily a condemnation of men and
women and only secondarily, and as an after-thought, exalta-
tion of God in his loving care for his children. The distortion has
been appalling; and in my view this distortion is one of the
reasons, although by no means the only or chief one, for the
rejection of Christian faith by so many people.

This is why I have been hesitant even to discuss the subject.
I believe that we should spend much more of our time in em-
phasizing what I have styled the positive side of the Christian
message, its proclamation of God as love, its insistence on
human sonship to God, its stress on the value of human activity
in the world, its hopefulness about the divine victory, above all
its central assertion that God in Christ has reconciled the world
to himself. And yet I have felt it necessary to turn to the question

of the wrongness in men and women, and this for a simple reason. A not inconsiderable number of writers on and critics of the type of theological reconstruction undertaken by process theologians like myself have said that we do not give sufficient attention to the evil in the world, above all to human sinfulness. They have said that we are too ready to talk about God as love and about the world as an ongoing process of creative advance, buying this belief (as one such critic has put it) altogether too cheaply. In another set of lectures, published as a book in Britain under the title *Goodness Distorted* (Mowbrays, 1970), I have tried to deal with this criticism so far as the general question of evil is concerned. Now I have sensed the need for a similar effort in respect to the fact of *human* wrongness; and however inadequate this effort may turn out to have been, at least it represents an attempt to show how seriously a process theologian can take the ugly side of human nature in all that goes contrary to the purpose of God for human wholeness.

Because this is so, it will be necessary to speak at some length about the general position taken by those of us who accept the process conceptuality. With that I must associate some of the valuable insights of existentialism, since I believe that the latter gives us what Teilhard de Chardin called "the inside" of the story, just as the process view gives us what he styled "the outside." The two can go together in this area, if nowhere else—although I agree with Schubert Ogden that they fit nicely in many other areas, too.

But first of all we must say something about the biblical material and its place in the picture. What would a process theologian say about Scripture? Let me begin by insisting that the Bible is for all Christians the normative element in the tradition of which they are a part; more will be said about that in the second chapter. It holds its place because in its pages we are given the story of the activity of God in history, set in the context of the natural creation. This activity reaches its culmination in the appearance of Jesus and the emergence of the specific response to him that constitutes Christian faith itself. Whatever may be its value as "literature", even as "religious literature", the point of the Christian appeal to Scripture is in its

telling the story of that activity of God. The telling is in a variety
of ways—there is history, poetry, legal enactment, legend,
myth, even apparently nonreligious material like the Book of
Esther where the word "God" is not mentioned; there is theology too. The various elements must be interpreted in a fashion
appropriate to the material: legend as legend, poetry as poetry,
history as history, theology as theology. And the methodology
employed in the whole enterprise should be that employed for
any other material coming to us from ancient times; we dare not
treat the Bible as if it were dropped from heaven and entirely
different from every other piece of literature.

A right approach to Scripture demands that we avoid the
tendency to get ourselves bogged down in minute details and
that we do not handle any single section in isolation from the
rest. A former teacher of mine used to insist that we should look
for what he called "the main lines of development, the major
emphases, and the implications" of what we read. Naturally we
find all these in and under the circumstances familiar to the
compilers and writers of the material. Sometimes the idiom used
is so "dated" that it seems quite incredible. But what is required
of us is an enduring effort to identify ourselves with the patterns
of thought and the ways of expression that material reflects.
Such identification is not the same as naive acceptance of things
as they are represented; it is not a literal approach but an
imaginative one. Hence insight, empathy, and sympathetic
penetration into significance through particular episodes or
teaching are utterly essential. If we lack these our biblical study
will be wooden, without much use save on the textual side or in
the ordering of ideas *obviously* present in the text. These are
important, to be sure; yet the best biblical study is marked by an
imaginative identification that refuses to be tied to explicit
wording but gets inside the material and grasps what is *really*
being said, even when the idiom used is impossible for us to
accept.

Granted this approach, which most contemporary biblical
scholars adopt, the Bible remains normative for us. But it does
not remain *alone*. The Scriptures come to us in the context of a
living and developing tradition that includes much else. Wor-

ship, to take one example, provides part of that setting. Theological awareness provides another. The experience of prayer and the activity of Christian discipleship are also there. In other words, the Bible is the *Church's* book: the Old Testament for the Jewish community of faith, the Old and New Testaments together for the Christian community of faith. As the Church's book, the Bible is not a scientific manual; it is a guide to faith's discernment of God. That is why the scientific ideas of the writers are not important for us; in fact, they may seem absurd to us today. G. K. Chesterton may have exaggerated but he made a useful point when he remarked that "the Bible is not to teach us how the heavens go, but how to go to heaven." Of course "going to heaven" is not exactly the truth of the matter; it would have been better to say, with some sacrifice of clever phrasing, that the Bible is there to show us what God is up to in the world, what human existence is about, and how we may be related to the reality of God in the immediate situations in which we find ourselves at whatever time and in whatever place we happen to live.

We appeal to Scripture, but in no literalistic fashion. We are neither fundamentalists who dwell on the exact text, nor "neo-fundamentalists" who talk about infallible biblical types, motifs, or patterns, and whose method of interpretation irons out all the variety and complexity of the material the Bible contains in order to get at some single supposedly pervasive concept or idea. There *is* such a motif, to be sure; but that is not the way to come to it. And what is more, the appeal to the Bible must go hand in hand with some broader conceptuality that in our own day best helps us to understand the world in which we are now placed.

This use of a philosophical conceptuality has always been integral to the theological enterprise, although sometimes it has been without full awareness of the procedure. In the Patristic Age, there was the world view of the Hellenistic period, as when Clement and Origen accepted Middle Platonism or when St. Augustine accepted Neo-Platonism. In the Middle Ages, it was either the continuing Platonizing view or (with Thomas Aquinas and others) newly recovered Aristotelianism. Later on, still other conceptualities had their place. In the 19th century, for example, German theology was related first to Kantian and then to Hegelian thought, while English theology first used the empiricism of the period and later the idealism of the Oxford school. And despite the claim of some contemporary theologians that they are free from all "contamination by secular philosophy", much of neo-orthodoxy in its several representatives shows the influence of neo-Kantianism, existentialism, phenomenological analysis, or the linguistic philosophy of the Vienna Circle and the contemporary English school. One might even say that the *unconscious* employment of one or other of these views is all the more dangerous, since often the theologian is unaware of what he or she is doing and hence is uncritical in attitude. If we are going to have a relationship to some contemporary pattern of thought—and it is unavoidable that we do have such—it is much better to know what we are doing, why we are doing it, and how we can best (and most critically) use the pattern we have accepted as valuable and helpful.

For myself and many other contemporary theologians process philosophy seems the most adequate conceptuality available today. We do not pretend that it is otherwise; we are prepared to give reasons for what we are doing. Elsewhere I have attempted both to explain this kind of thinking and to give the case for a Christian use of it *(Process Thought and Christian Faith,* Macmillan, 1968). So have Schubert Ogden in *The Reality of God* (Harpers, 1967), John Cobb in *A Christian Natural Theology* (Westminster, 1965), Peter Hamilton in *The Living God and Modern World* (United Church Press, 1967), and Daniel Day Williams in *The Spirit and the Forms of Love* (Harpers, 1968). Primarily we all accept process thinking because we believe it is *true,* or as true as we are likely to find possible at this present time; secondarily, because it "fits" Christian faith better than any other available type—or so we believe.

Now the process conceptuality lays great stress on the dynamic, developmental, and societal interpretation of the world; and with the world, also of God and of humanity. I shall use this thought in later chapters and with it I shall associate some of the insights of existentialists as they speak of "what it feels like" to be human. In addition, there will be some reference to the contribution of psychology in respect to the structure and motivations of human experience; to the view of history that sees it not as a mere catalogue of past happenings but as an entrance in the present into the past that has made this present what it is; and to the stress on "the future" that is found in so much contemporary analysis of the human situation.

The need for taking into account these movements in modern thought ought to be apparent. It is absurd to suppose that our idea of human nature, in its every aspect, has not been altered enormously by other recent study. For one example, we may cite the increase in self-awareness that has been gained through the work of psychologists. The contribution of academic psychology has helped us to see the dynamic nature of human existence, with its movement towards the fulfilling of aims or goals; while the depth-psychologists, the psychiatrists, and those who work in the field of social psychology have modified, indeed largely revolutionized, our understanding of human motivation, emotional response, ways of personal integration, the place of environmental pressures from the culture in which we share, and the origin of distortions and twistings in personality.

To talk about "man", in the religious and theological perspective, without using such insights would be to talk about a nonexistent entity. When with this material we combine the knowledge we now possess about the more general setting of human life in an evolving world characterized by interrelationship at every level, we are given a quite new picture of what it means to be human. There is no denial of selfhood or the capacity for choice and free decision within certain limits; but even in this area we know a great deal more than our ancestors. Above all, we now find it impossible to see ourselves and others in the static terms so often used in earlier definitions of human nature.

When Thomas Aquinas took over from Boethius the definition of "man" as "an individual substance of a rational nature", he was pointing to a truth that needed stating. He was indicating both that there is no such thing as "manhood" in the abstract

sense and also that a characteristic quality of human existence is
its capacity for thought. Each of us is a "rational" creature. Yet
in defining human nature as he did, in terms acceptable in his
time and inevitable in the light of the knowledge then available,
no attention was given to the dynamic quality of human personality. Hence for us today such definitions are at best partial and
may be seriously misleading. Furthermore, the frequent use of
"individual" as part of the conventional definition leads to
misunderstanding, since to be "an individual" may mean that
one is but a single existent in a given class or category, quite
apart from relationships with others; hence the rich sociality of
concrete human actuality may be minimized or forgotten. We
require a more living portrayal as well as a more social one.

In rethinking the significance of sin, or human wrongness,
we shall arrive at a better understanding if we take full account
of this new knowledge. Above all we shall be delivered from the
danger of thinking that this fact of experience, whatever it turns
out to be, is a matter of discrete and isolated instances of human
behaviour. Such behaviour, in this or that specific act, reflects a
situation or state; and the latter has very wide implications whose
significance has not always been grasped.

I conclude this first chapter with an appeal for sympathetic
appreciation of what is being attempted in our study. It is worth
repeating, in view of likely misrepresentation, that we are not
seeking to evade the harsh fact the word "sin" is getting at. If the
traditional *concept* is today likely to be gravely misleading, as I
think it is, the reality to which it has pointed is even more
unfortunate and tragic. The horror of human defection from the
good, the spectacle of the wrongness in human existence, impo-
tence and frustration, deviation and distortion, are undeniable.
What we may wish to *call* this, how we may describe it, and the
setting in which we place it are nothing like so important as that
we honestly recognize it for what it is.

I also ask for a friendly awareness of the tentative nature of
the suggestions to be made in this book. Certainly nobody in his
right mind would suppose that in half-a-dozen chapters one can
exhaust the subject. Yet the attempt to make such suggestions
has its own importance too. Whatever is said in this study will be

said in loyalty to the deepest intention of the biblical view of humanity, even if the phraseology found in Scripture is not always employed and even when some details of the general biblical world view are said to be inadequate, imperfect, perhaps erroneous. What we are attempting is an interpretation of human wrongness that is faithful to that which the Bible is getting at.

I conclude by saying that today we should seek to be as radical as possible. But I remind my readers that "radical" derives from the Latin *radix*, which means "root." Our purpose should not be revolutionary, in the sense of trying to start entirely *de novo* as if we were beginning afresh. On the contrary, it should be to discover the root-meaning in the traditional concept and in the general biblical position it once effectively conveyed. The last thing that I desire is to participate in the easy game of sniping at our Christian forbears because they did not think or talk as we do. I am convinced that the way to be faithful to the tradition we inherit is not through a simple repetition of the traditional phrases, but by looking for the intention with which the phrases were used; with enormous respect for the insights of the past; with complete loyalty to the basic affirmations of Christian faith; and with generous openness to, and readiness to use, whatever new knowledge has been granted us.

2
Sin in Biblical Thought

We have already insisted that the central place of the Bible in the Christian tradition is not open to any doubt. It is the book that gives us the story of how we came to be what we are as Christians. The background of Christian faith in the long history of the Jewish people is found there. The account of the coming of Jesus Christ, a telling of the impressions remembered and handed on in oral tradition from those who had companied with him or knew about him from those who had enjoyed this privilege, is to be read there. The primary response to Jesus, with the initial consequences of his life, teaching, deeds, death, and rising-again, is told there. Without the Bible we should not know what Christianity is all about; we should be at the mercy of changing fashions in thought and belief, lacking any standard by which we could judge development as sound or unsound, right or wrong, good or bad.

But as we have also said earlier, this should not suggest to us that the Scriptures are to be used as if they were a mine from which we might dig suitable proof-texts, or as a convenient encyclopaedia in which we might discover exactly what we ought to think and believe. Like any collection of writings that has come into existence over a long period of time, the Bible contains very diversified material. There are contradictions within it that make impossible a simple appeal to its supposedly explicit and precise teaching. In their own way the English Reformers recognized this when they said in the Anglican Thirty-Nine Articles that no one place in Scripture is to be interpreted in a way inconsistent with the rest. In a manner of speaking this is an opening of the door to proper critical study of the Scriptures, although those reformers were hardly aware of doing this.

The various parts of the Bible must be read in the light of the conditions under which they were set down. As people wrote about what had happened to them (or about anything else, for that matter), they naturally did their writing in the way appropriate to their time and place. Their science was not ours; the way in which they saw things, the concepts they inherited and used, the ideas that were in the air, inevitably had their effect both upon their own understanding and also on their actual writing. It could not be otherwise if they were human, not automatic machines for reproducing something thrust upon them from outside.

Thus we cannot speak of the "inspiration of Holy Scripture" as if it meant a removal of the human factors that played their part in giving us the biblical material. Nor should most of us be prepared to think that the Bible *as a book* is inspired in such an extraordinary fashion. We should speak about the persons who did the writing and how they were brought to stress the reality of God, his self-disclosure in the events of history, the response made to this disclosure, the salvatory consequences that followed, and the importance that was found in that ongoing movement. Some of us, perhaps, would agree with Dr. R.P.C. Hanson who has urged, in an essay in *The Attractiveness of God* (London, S.P.C.K., 1973), that the concept of "inspiration" is no longer tenable and that in its place we should speak of the Bible as "unique" precisely because it gives us the formative, hence the normative, account of what Christianity as a faith in God professes to be. Here, Dr. Hanson argues, is the record of how the people of Israel, and later the earliest Christian community, responded to what they believed to be God's particular and decisive action in world history, through a given people who lived in a given part of the world and who for hundreds or thousands of years were profoundly convinced of God's action with them and for them.

Since they centre in Jesus, the Scriptures in their Christian use have a very special importance. The development of the Jewish response to God's activity finds its climax in what took place in Palestine in "the reign of Tiberius Caesar, Pontius Pilate being governor of Judaea." God acts in all history and in the natural realm too, but we believe that at that time and in that place he acted with peculiar intensity. What prepared for that moment, what went on in and around it, and what has followed after it, constitute the point of Christian faith. Nobody can doubt the accuracy of Hanson's claim that the supreme importance of Scripture is found, for Christians, exactly there.

So much for our general approach to the Bible. The specific concern of this chapter is with what the Bible has to tell us about the wrongness in human existence.

What does the Bible say about sin? Obviously this is not the place for a complete, even an adequate, survey of the biblical material on the subject. The best we can do is to consider the main points, the thrust as we might say, of biblical literature. And the first thing to say is that in its essential purpose the Bible is not "about sin" at all; it is about God and God's relationship with his people as this found its focus first in the Jewish nation and then most pointedly in "the Man of God's own choosing." The Bible has to do with God. It is about what he has done, what he is doing, and what he will do, and all this in relationship with his creation, his human children, the Jewish people, and this or that particular man and woman. Whatever else the Bible says is a corollary or application or consequence following from its main concern.

Yet it is true that the Bible *does* speak about human wrongness or sin. It does this in connexion with its central message; but it does it, nonetheless. Here I wish to suggest three points, each of which will have its relevance in our discussion. The three may be listed as follows:

1. The Bible tells us that the human situation is one in which God's perfect will is not obeyed. Hence there is something wrong about this situation.

2. The Bible tells us that this situation extends to include each and every one of us. In telling this, it represents us as alienated from God's purpose and estranged both from him and from each other.

3. The Bible tells us that each and every one decides for

himself or herself, with a responsibility that cannot be handed over to anybody else, to think and speak and act in ways that are wrong—and wrong because they are contrary to God's perfect will and hence are displeasing to him and damaging to other persons.

We must say something about each of these points. First, however, we need to consider what the biblical material means when it speaks of what we have just styled, in our own idiom, God's perfect will or his purpose. What sort of God is it with whom we have to do, whose will or purpose we are to fulfil, and failure to fulfil whose will or purpose is (as we have put it) "wrong"?

The scriptural picture of God is not a matter of some philosophical idea or concept. It is drawn from what has been known in the experience of a people and of those who belonged to this people. The God about whom we read in Scripture is no "unmoved mover", "absolute being", "first cause". He is indeed the mover of the world, supreme and perfect; he is the chief cause, although not the only cause in the world. But he is pictured as the transcendently righteous One, with resources adequate for carrying out his plan; as the transcendently good One, whose "power" is chiefly manifest "in mercy and pity", as a prayer book collect phrases it; as the transcendently loving One who cares for and identifies himself with his creation and his human children in the creation—an insight that grew gradually through the years about which the Old Testament tells and finally flowered in the response made to what Jesus was and said, did and meant.

As transcendently—and by this word I mean inexhaustibly, indefatigably, and indefeasibly supreme and perfect, and *not* remote or aloof or self-contained—righteous, good, and loving, God is seen always in relationship with the world and in communication of himself to that world. He works in it and through it, unfailingly and unceasingly, to accomplish a purpose or to fulfil an intention that, like his own character, must be righteous, good, and loving. Where that intention or purpose is operative, *there* God is present; hence the divine transcendence is balanced by divine immanence. Yet let us be sure that we do not think of those two terms in some *abstract* metaphysical sense but in the *concrete* metaphysical sense that has to do with genuine actualities and with generalizations from actual experience.

The perfect intention or purpose of God is to share with his creation the righteousness, goodness, and love that are his own nature. It will be expressed through working for us to live one with another and with him in justice, in unfailing concern, and with the love that relates itself to, and shares with, others in all that it has and is. This means that for us to live in accordance with God's will and purpose is for us to be in just relations with others, to manifest the goodness that is unfailing concern, and to live and act in loving awareness. Failure to live and to act in that way is to disobey God, to displease him. That is the human situation as we now know and experience it and as we now share in it, precisely because we are all members one of another.

We may now turn to a further discussion of the three points I listed above: (1) There is something wrong with the human situation; (2) This wrongness is a social fact inclusive of all men and women; (3) Each of us is responsible for the choices he or she makes that are specific acts of wrong-doing, wrong-thinking, wrong-speaking.

First, then, the wrongness of the human situation. This situation is wrong because it is not in accordance with God's will—and we must remember that here we have to do with no artificially imposed law but precisely with God's ever-present activity to promote good. Not only is the situation wrong because God's will *should* be done; it is wrong because God's will *could* be done. In the Bible the reality of human freedom is never denied. For the Bible it is entirely possible that in this real freedom men and women *might* so have acted and lived that, instead of being wrong, things might have been right. Evil in the broader sense and sin in the narrower human sense of wrong are neither intended nor predestined by God himself—his will is always perfect in its righteousness, its goodness, and its love. That is why the situation is so tragic. It is a dreadful distortion of the way things should have gone and could have gone.

No biblical writer minimizes this tragic quality nor the

seriousness of the situation. No matter what may be his theory of how the situation has come to be, the fact of it in its seriousness and tragedy is never forgotten. The condition of the human race, in what we shall soon see to be its alienation and estrangement, does not present a pretty spectacle. If the Bible is not pessimistic about things, it most surely is realistic about them.

Secondly, we see the social solidarity of men and women in this wrongness. What is true of the situation as a whole affects each of us who by virtue of our social belonging is participant in that situation.

In recent years biblical students have come to see ever more clearly that the Scriptures do not talk about the sort of individualism in which each man or woman is an isolated monad. On the contrary, they tell us of a belonging-together, in which there is mutual influence, common sharing, genuine participation of each in others. Some scholars have spoken of the concept of "corporate personality" as the only way in which we can state this biblical view. Maybe that concept, as such, is too extreme. It does point to the truth, however; and we may phrase that truth in biblical texts that tell us that we are "knit together" in a "bundle of life."

To say with the prophets, "The soul that sinneth, it shall die", is not to contradict this social belonging and influence. As our third point will make clear, to speak in that fashion is to emphasize the responsibility of each of us for our wrongness in thought, word, and deed; but so to speak does not negate the main thrust of the biblical witness, that we are members one of another and that we are "incorporated" into the human race with all our brethren. All are thus "in Adam", as Paul tells us—members of the body of humankind, with no one of us existing to, for, and of the self alone.

Occasionally this truth is put in an oddly biological way: "In sin hath my mother conceived me." The wrongness here has nothing to do with sexuality, about which (with some occasional blind spots) Jewish thought was extraordinarily hospitable and healthy. What is intended is that the human situation *is* wrong and that everyone who is conceived and born is a sharer in that wrongness. It might equally well have been said that "in sin I am writing these pages", or equally, "in sin my readers are reading these pages." If the situation is wrong, then all who are involved in it—and that means everyone, without exception—is "in the wrong." Furthermore, the wrongness means an alienation from God that is damaging to each person and painful to God; it means estrangement or separation from each other and from God.

Again, let us admit that these two words, "alienation" and "estrangement", are not biblical, although in the Pauline epistles we read about our being "alienated" from God, while we also hear of our being "enemies" of God. Nonetheless, what the terms signify was clear enough to the biblical writers. Insofar as, and to the degree that, we share in the social situation that is contrary to the divine purpose and will and therefore wrong, we are alien to that purpose and will and are estranged from, by being disobedient to, the perfection of righteousness, goodness, and love that is God himself and that it is our own genuinely human purpose to express in creaturely ways.

Third, each of us is responsible for decisions made for or against God's purpose and will. When left to ourselves, we tend to decide for that which it is wrong for us to choose. This is a matter of observable fact. In so doing, we affect others too, by reason of our solidarity with them, and therefore augment the wrongness of the total situation and the consequent alienation and estrangement.

Human solidarity does not diminish the responsibility of each man or woman for his or her own decisions. We cannot claim that we "could not help it" when we have made the wrong decision. There may seem to be a paradox here, but to the biblical writers it did not seem so; what they were doing was simply stating both sides of a single fact. We are all sharers in a situation that has affected us seriously and tragically because it is wrong; at the same time, each one has a degree of freedom that enables him or her to decide for himself or herself on this or that particular course of action. The biblical writers did not try to reconcile these two statements of fact; they put them down and believed that both were true—and I believe that we can say that ordinary experience bears them out.

Of course, freedom of decision has its limits; we shall speak about this at a later stage. For the moment let us recognize that deep within us there is a sense of responsibility that makes us feel guilty when we have chosen that which we know to be less than the best possible under the circumstances. This is an indelible part of our human experience, as existentialist analysis has made clear enough.

In each one of us, the biblical witness tells us, there is a desire to obtain immediately satisfying results or a good that is obvious and readily available. There is also a tendency to want one's own way without regard for others or for the long-range consequences of our choice. It is therefore almost "natural," in one sense of that word, for each person to act wrongly. He or she *might* have done otherwise, but has preferred the second best, the lesser good, because it appealed to him, attracted her, and seemed satisfying in its immediacy. What is more, these choices may conflict with those of other people. To what degree, then, are we prepared to recognize this fact and make the necessary accommodations?

Whatever I do I must accept responsibility—failure here is a refusal to act like a human person who is possessed both of rationality and of freedom. But the consequences of my decisions are not for myself only; they influence others. Thus my decisions for the wrong augment the general wrongness and make it all the more serious for others who are impeded in *their* decisions because of what mine have brought about. Contrariwise, right decisions on my part make it more likely that others will choose rightly.

Tied in with these three basic points about wrongness, the Bible tells us that none of us is a desembodied spirit or simply another animal. We are body-mind, whose physical or sensible experience is organically one with our mental or psychological experience. In any decisions we make, the whole of us is involved. While it is through decisions by the will, made in response to attractions known to the mind, that we do whatever we do, the whole of us is in the picture. We are made of "the dust of the earth", upon which God has "breathed spirit"; so we have become living entities. If we were just "of the earth", we would be like the "beasts that perish"; if we were just "spirit", we would be like angels. Instead we are both sense and spirit, organic entities; and neither body nor soul, separately, can be taken to be the self. We are *flesh,* historically embodied, physically embodied, part of the natural order, *but with a difference* since we are also conscious, possessed of reason, and able to articulate our desires and drives.

Nobody can "save" himself or herself; only God can do that. To explore the soteriological question—how humankind is given the grace or enabling favour to live in accordance with the divine purpose or will and find thereby true fulfillment and authentic personhood—would be to begin another study. At the moment and for our present purpose, the reason for introducing God's activity in "saving" or "making whole" is to bring still another biblical emphasis to our attention. This has to do with the human relationship with God.

We have seen that the human situation is somehow wrong, that all of us are involved in the wrongness because we are participant in the human race, and that each one by concrete decisions both can and does contribute to the situation in which he or she finds himself or herself. For the Bible the heart of the matter is that in all these ways human relationship goes wrong. That is why we could use the words "alienation" and "estrangement", for these are words that have to do with relationship.

Now our difficulty is that human relationship has gone wrong not only among us men and women but also in respect to God himself. We are not related as we ought to be and might be with God; the consequence is that we are not related as we ought to be and might be with our fellows. That may seem strange; but the point is that when we see that God *is* the Love that works in the world to bind us together in righteousness, goodness, and love, we also see that a violation of that righteousness, goodness, and love (wherever found) is essentially "against" God and is expressed visibly and plainly "against" our fellow men and women. Thus we may say that for the Bible, when we come to its deepest teaching, sin is understood as violation of, damage done to, and deprivation in a relationship between God and his children and hence also between and among men and women. The human situation in its seriousness and tragedy is a result of this distorted or deviant or violated or damaged relationship. So too in our personal decisions and our personal wrongness, the basic problem is the violation of the intentional relationship of the person to God and hence of person to person. To put it in simplest terms, to sin is against God because it is against the fellowship God purposes for us with himself and with our brethren.

So far we have said nothing about the distinctively New Testament addition to the general biblical picture, an addition that radically alters the way in which that picture should be understood. The first element in that addition is what might be styled the interiorization of the understanding of the human situation and of each person's wrongness. In his teaching Jesus was intent on doing just this. It was in the "heart of man" that the trouble lay; and because it lay there, we now can see the situation in a different fashion. The sayings of Jesus about the eye that offends, about the one who "in his heart" hates or lusts, and so much else in his remembered words are all indicative of this interiorizing. What Jesus is saying is that what is wrong about us and our situation is deeper than mere violation; it is in attitude and desire and emotional awareness. Our inner spirit has gone wrong; our outward acts are the visible expression of that inner condition. This is why love, and love alone, can remedy things; only love can penetrate to our very heart or spirit and win our response.

In the second place, the whole impact of Jesus, quite as much as his remembered teaching, led the first Christians to see with peculiar clarity that this love is the clue to everything about human life, as well as to God's own nature and action. The word "love" is a dangerous one, for it is open to serious misunderstanding. It can be taken to mean sentimentality or "niceness", just as it can be thought to refer only to animal lust. The word *agape* in New Testament usage—and not without an impressive Old Testament background in the term *chesed* or "loving-kindness"—signifies neither sentimentality nor lust, but rather outward-going, open-hearted, self-giving concern and care, readiness to suffer as well as to share delight, the giving of self to others, hopefulness about possibilities in those others. Indeed it describes a mutuality, giving-and-receiving, faithfulness, and a commitment that is enriching and strengthening. Love like that is what *God* is: God *is* love. And wherever love of that quality is found, there God is at work; he is "pure unbounded love" in himself and in his activity. He wishes his creation, above all his human children, to share in that love.

Hence, between persons, between all human lives, there is to be that "love and charity" that reflects the divine lovingkindness. Righteousness, upon which the Old Testament has been so insistent both in respect to God's purpose and to the human mode of social existence, is basically an expression of such love. To call God good is to say that he aims at bringing others to participate in this love that itself is so *very* good.

When this love is stressed, we can see that the *real* difficulty with the human situation in its serious and tragic wrongness is that love is *not* shared there, as it should be and could be—as in God's purpose it is meant to be shared. We can also see that the *real* difficulty with each wrong decision is grounded in failure to realize oneself as the lover that each was intended to be. As a matter of fact, for the whole biblical witness sin against God and sin against one's neighbour are linked together; what Jesus does is to make this patently clear, so clear that the picture is now seen in a fresh light.

It is important also to observe that the wrongnesses about which the Bible is most explicit are in what we should call the secular realm. Each of us can and does set himself or herself up as "master of all he surveys" and thus blasphemously tries to usurp God's place in the scheme of things. That is true; yet it is to be noted that the way in which this outrageous pride manifests itself practically is through over-weening, arrogant, thoughtless, careless, and contemptuous attitudes towards and actions among one's fellow men and women. This is the explanation of the deep concern of the prophets when they see social injustice, mistreatment of the poor and needy, self-satisfaction at the expense of others, and callousness and cruelty. It is also the explanation of Jesus' reaction when he saw such things in his own time and place and when he spoke out so plainly about these matters.

In this discussion of the biblical view of sin I have not attempted to bolster my argument by an extended citation of texts. For what it is worth, let me say that I am convinced that the summary I have given is true enough to the biblical material, once one grants the difference in language and the necessity of placing the several points in our contemporary setting. Leonard Hodgson, sometime professor of theology at Oxford, was accustomed to use a phrase that ran something like this: "What must the case be, if people who wrote and thought like that, in their own time and place, spoke about it in the way in which they did?" That is, he urged what might be styled a "proportional" interpretation of the biblical witness. Dr. Hodgson yielded to none in his desire to take Scripture as the norm for Christian thinking, but he was ahead of his time in seeing that the appeal to Scripture is not to be conceived as if one were consulting a dictionary or a collection of quotations. That would have been a misuse of the Bible. Christians, he used to say, were supposed to believe that the Spirit would "take of the things" our fathers said and thought; and through those things would "lead us" into an ever-deeper awareness of truth. Such was my former teacher's way of approach; I believe he was supremely right and I have sought to follow his path.

In the remaining chapters we shall attempt to suggest ways in which we can best do this job. If the concept of sin seems meaningless to many today, the facts to which it pointed are with us still—obviously and terribly with us. Perhaps a rather different approach to, portrayal of, and wrestling with those facts may help to make our non-believing friends see this. At any rate, nobody ought to be able to accuse us of making light of those facts nor of failing to take most seriously that with which our fathers in the Christian faith were so deeply concerned: what is wrong in human life and the human situation. That something *is* terribly and tragically wrong only the foolish or the blind would dare to deny.

3
Existential Analysis and Process Thought

I shall now seek to give a summary statement of the conceptuality that, as it seems to me, is most helpful in our time. I refer, of course, to process thought. But before that summary I wish to consider the contribution made to our understanding of human existence by that group of thinkers who may be given the name "existentialists" —although there are great differences in detail and opinion among them. Heidegger, Jaspers, Camus, Marcel, Sartre, to name the more important, are all influenced to a large extent by the work of the Danish writer Søren Kierkegaard, but they do not agree in their own formulations and I can do no more than take what appear to me the chief points in their "over-all" view and seek to state them briefly.

Yet what does seem to me obvious is that there is a remarkable, if somewhat unconscious, convergence of existentialism, so understood, and of process thinking. With these two I should couple much that is said by the psychologists, psychoanalysts, and psychiatrists, although I cannot pretend to be an expert here and shall not try to present their views save by an occasional allusion. The convergence of which I am speaking is by way of telling us that we shall understand existence, human or otherwise, only in terms of dynamic activity towards goals more or less consciously accepted. As I have said before, there is an "inside" story the existentialists and the psychologists give us, and there is also an "outside" story that process thinking provides.

However this may be, in the present chapter I shall begin with a sketch of the existentialist view of human nature and then proceed to a summary of process thought, and towards the end include some remarks about the results of psychological work as represented by analysts and therapists of the "depth" school. Finally I shall attempt to spell out in more detail the relevance of all this to the Christian understanding of human personality in community, with special reference to the light that is thrown upon the wrongness in the human situation and in each of us as we decide, for good or for ill, to live and act towards the realization of our human possibility. To attempt all this in a single chapter means that what will be said must of necessity be far from exhaustive; once again, I am presuming only to make suggestions that others may wish to take up or that they may reject as erroneous or misleading.

Both process thought and existentialism—and depth psychology too, for that matter—are agreed that human life is dynamic. It is movement towards a goal; it is the striving to actualize potentialities and thereby to find satisfaction or fulfillment. Perhaps this is the best point to begin, then. Let us turn to the existentialist analysis of human existence, speaking as it does so directly to the concrete "felt" experience of men and women.

In most traditional thinking, the essence of a thing was considered to be prior to and more important than its existence. *Thatness* or "manhood" took precedence over *whatness* or this specific and experienced quality or awareness in this particular person. Thus "manhood" was taken to be definable in an abstract way; and whatever was to be said about this or that person in his and her concrete actuality as human was derivative from the prior conception of the essence *"manhood."* Thus there were established norms or patterns or (in the popular phrase) "ideals of manhood", to which actual existence was conformed with greater or less adequacy. "What is man?" it was asked; and the use of the verb *is* at once indicated that essence, or being (substance), gave to human "becoming" whatever meaning it might possess. Obviously in a finite and created world like ours and with due consideration of the sort of creatures we are, there was change. "Becoming" was an *aspect* of creation, but it was less real than "being" and always marked by imperfection and lack. The "really real" was above and beyond and other than change with its supposed "imperfection."

The existentialist position reverses this whole outlook. What we know and what we experience, it tells us, is our own existence; and that existence is patently a matter of our becoming and not of our being. Existence precedes essence, not the other way round. The concrete actuality not only of human life but of everything else in the world comes before whatever we may feel obliged to say concerning the "isness" of things. Indeed, the existentialist is prepared to urge that so far as we hope to speak significantly about things, including ourselves, we must see that the only genuine "isness" that is theirs is in fact their becoming. For we know nothing about, nor have we any way of gaining access to, an imagined "ideal perfection" that is above all change, development, or movement. Furthermore, the notion that the changeless alone is definable as perfect, while by necessity of definition anything that changes must be imperfect, is taken by the existentialist to be an arbitrary assumption—historically understandable in the light of Greek and other philosophical ideas, to be sure, but without any adequate demonstration and running clean contrary to our own experience as living existents in the only world we know.

In the existentialist picture, our inner subjectivity must therefore have a very central place. We look into ourselves as we know ourselves to be, as living, feeling, developing creatures; this is the "subjective pathos" that is what we know at first hand. From grasping the significance of this experience of our subjectivity, we learn that each of us has been "thrown into the world", without any choice made by us; each exists here and now and nowhere else and each must accept existence in just that way. None of us is here, however, as a "finished article." Each is here as a dynamic thrust towards the future. In each the stuff of existence is redeemed from being *mere* stuff by projective aim or purposive intention. As Sartre has said, it is distinctive of human existence that it has a *pour-soi* or projected selfhood at which it aims; this saves it, once it is accepted and lived out in such terms, from being only *en-soi* or a characterless lump that can be called "mere" existence. But each must do this for himself or herself since each finds his or her true project *as an individual* and not as belonging to the commonality of the race. Thus there is a stress upon particularity, as I should prefer to put it; we ought to talk about *men* and *women*, each of them with a specific existence, rather than about human kind en masse. Kierkegaard warned against "the public" or the "mass-man"; for him that amorphous public "manhood" was a menace to the integrity of each person's genuine selfhood.

Since each person must decide for himself or herself to accept an aim and to project existence towards a future possibility, the existentialist lays great emphasis on the necessity for commitment or "engagement." If there is any one factor in the existentialist picture that has attracted attention, it is just here. The insistence on decision or commitment is absolutely central. Apart from this there can be no authenticity of life. Each of us becomes authentically himself or herself as and when he or she commits himself or herself to the future self that he or she is to realize; and in so doing commits himself or herself to the particular project or cause that each determines to serve. That project or cause may be self-centred and narrow; it may be other-centred (Sartre would perhaps deny this) and open. It is certainly bound to be relative rather than absolute, although it makes absolute claims on the one who commits himself or herself. Through such commitment each one is moved to actualize more fully the selfhood that is potentially his or her own project.

Yet many of not all existentialists are also conscious of our social milieu and find that this belonging with our fellows is part of human existence. This is a "with-world", as Heidegger has told us; we exist with others, related intimately to them in a fashion that does not deny but augments our own selfhood. Those who think like Sartre find this both embarrassing and difficult, since to them "other people" can only be seen as "the enemy." That is to say, this or that person with whom I am necessarily related in the social milieu poses a threat to the realization of my own specific possibility, and I pose a threat to the other in similar fashion. Other people are "hell"; and not only other people, but even physical things as they impose upon us the frightening requirements that we take account of them and somehow accommodate ourselves to their being here with us. We may feel a need to conform to their demands upon us and thus lose our own identity. Even then, however, we may still "choose our freedom"; and in spite of, if not because of, the other person or the external world become authentic in our existence.

Gabriel Marcel and certain other existentialists take a more cheerful view of the situation. For them relationship with others is not a threat, save when we let it become so; primarily, it is an opportunity for enriched and enriching participation or sharing, whereby a finer and better self may be authentically realized by each of those concerned. Thus Marcel sees the family as providing a setting for sound and healthy development of each person's own existence. He thinks that it is in our sharing, and there above all, that we become genuinely human. Love through sharing, sharing in love, is the way to growth; and Marcel refuses to accept the cynical Sartrian notion that in intimate relationships, such as sexual union, we are engaged only in battle one with *an* other, or one with others, in an effort to overcome them and possess them for our own ends. On the contrary, thinks Marcel, these intimate relationships are our most human and most rewarding experiences. Even Sartre, it might be noted, must recognize that some measure of cooperation is necessary among us; but for him this is more like an enforced agreement on the part of those who are shipwrecked and must either help each other or die one by one, than it is like a family or community where each person knows that his or her own fulfillment is dependent upon that of others. Marcel is sure (and I believe rightly) that other people are worthy of affection and concern, both for their own sakes and also because they with us are together in a process of personality in the making.

Heidegger has said that human existence in the world with others is *towards death*. Only by accepting the inescapable fact of our mortality can our human aim have any radically significant sense. Some existentialists, however, while acknowledging this obvious truth, wish to say something more, especially those who have Christian convictions. Nonetheless, all would agree that unless we take our mortality with utmost seriousness, anything further (such as resurrection or eternal life in God) will be frivolous and unrealistic. We must not live in a fool's paradise and pretend that what happens to us in our span of life in this world is relatively unimportant. We all die; that is known to everybody. But that *all of us* dies, in every aspect of our existence, has not been admitted so generally. Yet unless we acknowledge this, we are deluding ourselves. If we do acknowledge it, the further meaning of our existence is "in spite of" (to use a Tillichian phrase) our mortality and must be a gift of God.

Again, the existentialist tells us that all truth of deep concern to us must be such that it is known with what Kierkegaard styled "subjective pathos" or deep personal association and grasping. Of course in technological matters, in scientific description, and the like, we may properly speak of a certain "objectivity", since we are not so enormously implicated in these matters. But when it comes to our deepest interest, our "ultimate concern", as Tillich used to say, we are necessarily subjective. Truth is known to us in our profound sense of commitment; it is not a matter of supposedly independent propositions or ideas that we consider in cold detachment. At this point the place where we stand or the context in which our existence is lived out has its part in determining our attitude; and such truth is given to us "existentially", not in terms of abstract "essences" or concepts.

In all this, the stress is not only on becoming and on movement and development but also on the direction of each person's existence as he or she aims for the realization of the possibilities open before him and her and the making actual of the potentialities that are part of each person's very stuff. The same line is adopted by process thinkers, and it is to them that we now turn our attention. We may even say that process thought provides a broader metaphysic in terms of which such an understanding of felt human existence can make sense.

But that statement must not be misunderstood. Metaphysics in *this* mode is not the same as that of the older philosophies. A process thinker does not claim that by a strenuous effort of the mind he can arrive at a world view in which everything in the cosmos is explained and all is given point and significance by a superterrestrial reality that (in contrast to the world of our experience) is immutable, impassible, and absolute in every respect. The process thinker is keenly aware of the "demon of the absolute", as Dr. Paul Elmer More once put it when he was discussing this pursuit, described by so many practitioners of metaphysics, of the entirely "beyond-the-world" being who is first and only cause and himself entirely self-contained and unaffected by anything else.

Metaphysics in the new mode is to be understood differently. It is the metaphysical task to look at oneself and the world, to attempt to find some aspect or factor that is so "important" (to use Whitehead's word) that it may provide a clue to how things go in the cosmos, and then to generalize that factor or aspect of experienced reality in order to see how far the generalization may apply to whatever else is open to experience and reflection. The result will always be tentative and not absolutely conclusive. It is not a question of constructing some all-inclusive system that will explain everything without remainder, nor of arriving by sheer logic at the necessity for an other-worldly entity whose existence provides such explanation. Rather, it is the effort to get some "vision of reality" that sufficiently comprehends the initial data and offers an insight into such other data as we know. This vision may then be taken as a clue to how things work, but not as claiming to be more than a valuable—and so far as may be, demonstrated—hypothesis that is subject to continued testing and hence is open to revision. Metaphysics in this mode is more modest than that in the older style; but it is metaphysics nonetheless, since it goes beyond (although it is always reliant upon) the grasp we have of human experience alone and is prepared to talk of the necessary "principles" expressed in that experience and in the wider reaches of the world. What it is seeking is a view that will be as inclusive as possible of as many of the facts as human experience and reflection make available to us.

The starting point, therefore, is in what it is like, what it feels like, what it entails, to be an experiencing human agent. Here it is inevitable that "becoming" will be the keyword for an understanding of the world, since that is what we know in ourselves. And becoming is tied in with process—that is, with movement towards aims or goals. The word "process" is used because Alfred North Whitehead, the "founding father" (although not without precursors) of this conceptuality employed it in calling his Gifford lectures *Process and Reality*: "The process *is* the reality", as he himself did say.

Why, it may be asked, have so many thinkers in the past assumed that somehow it is "less good" to "become" than to "be"? Why has perfection been taken to imply changelessness? Why has it been thought that "pure act", *actus purus,* to use the scholastic medieval phrase for completely fulfilled actuality in which there is no possibility of enrichment, must be regarded as superior to all movement, all development, and all enrichment through growth? The answer would seem to be that in Greek thought (and elsewhere too) it was simply axiomatic that change was necessarily associated with decay. The hymn puts it: "Change *and decay* in all around I see." This notion then embedded itself in later philosophy and was taken as an unquestioned and unquestionable truth, despite the patent fact that in our own experience of the world "to live is to change", as Cardinal Newman once remarked. Of course there is genuine truth in the ideas of stability and permanence, but these may be secured through change and growth without sacrificing the latter in any way.

The world we know is in process through becoming; there is a dynamic thrust towards the fulfillment of potentiality, with the emergence of genuine novelty. This is true in human existence, so that the occasions of experience of which each of us is "made up", like all other actual entities or energy-events in the creation, follow a routing or take a direction from unfulfilled possibility towards satisfaction through the making actual of what is potential. An initial aim is given, to be sure. This is brought into existence from the various prior energy-events, with the use of materials from the past; it is new, yet continuous with what has gone before. Influenced by other entities which it grasps and by which it is grasped, affected by the pressures upon it from the environment, each event aims at fulfillment because it has accepted the initial aim as the subjective goal for whose realization the entity strives. This initial aim, now become sub-jective end, provides a focus for the cosmos at this or that moment. The particular entity is lured towards its aim, yet it may decide negatively as well as positively and may (or may not) move to fulfillment in the right direction of advance.

That which we know in ourselves as the "emotional inten-sity" of experience is found, in its degree and manner, everywhere else in the creation. It may seem silly to say that an electron, for example, is processive in this way; but that is the case only if we presume that it is identical with, rather than analagous to, what we know ourselves to be like. Straight through the cosmos there is decision for or against aim, although this is not conscious decision in *our* sense. At every level, too, there is what I like to style the societal fact: in Whitehead's word, the world is *organismic*. Everything affects and is affected by everything else; there is no "simple location" without rela-tionship to other events. Nothing is completely discrete, iso-lated, or separated from its environment. The various influences or pressures, the graspings or "prehensions", are focused in a specific *here* and *now*; but their ramifications are far-reaching and eventually include the whole universe.

Thus the world is a social process, a world of relationships in which each participates in all and all have their influence upon each. Ultimately it is this actuality of energy-events *in process of actualization,* with the societal quality attaching to them all, that moves the world on to the future. And it is persuasion, rather than coercion, that is the chief mode of advance. Persuasion, or the lure and enticement towards satisfaction of aim, is deepest in the cosmos; this is because sheer force is self-defeating in the long run, however successful it may seem in the short one. This is why process thought is prepared to say that *love,* not omnipo-tent power, is the basic thrust or drive. For love is relationship in persuasion, with each event or entity helping other events or entities to realize their potentiality in an enriched society; where that does not happen, the creative advance is impeded, held back, or made to follow deviant or distorted paths. In the next chapter we shall see what is to be said about evil and human wrongness or sin in that context. Here I need only emphasize that process thought fully recognizes the tragic facts of evil and wrongness, although it does not find helpful the conventional accounts of these nor the explanations that have often been given for their presence in the creation. What makes evil a *problem* is precisely the horrifying contrast it presents to the augmenting of good in the world; how we deal with the problem is a different matter.

As each event moves towards realization, it must make decisions. The word "decision" is derived from a Latin word meaning "to cut off"; thus each event "cuts off" some possibilities in the very act of choosing others. The "continuum of possibility", as Peter Hamilton has well phrased it, cannot be given full and actual expression at any one moment in any one particular event or entity; this or that possibility must be selected from the infinite range of possibilities and from among the relevant opportunities. In human experience we know that we often make these decisions with less than a high degree of conscious awareness of what we are doing; yet we also know that there are times when we do have just such a high degree of awareness. We select this or that possibility presented to us because at the moment it seems that the one chosen will more adequately lead to what we take for the fulfillment of our aim; but often enough we are sadly mistaken in our selection. An analogous element of decision runs everywhere through the creation. In us, as we believe, there is a fuller sense of what is going on; and this is taken to be the clue to what happens elsewhere, since it makes sense of, and gives sense to, other things in this kind of world.

Existentialists are concerned largely with human experience and have little to say about the natural order or the cosmos at large. They interest themselves in the implications of immediate self-awareness and self-analysis. Process thinkers have a wider view. They are convinced that in such self-awareness and self-analysis we are given an insight into the natural order and the cosmos at large. Nowhere does this become so apparent as in the way in which the religious element in experience is interpreted. The existentialist will speak of the "Thou" who addresses the human subject and to whom that subject makes response. So will the process thinker. The latter will also speak of God as the One met in such an "encounter". But he or she is sure that if there is validity in religious experience and if life's significance requires trustworthiness in the structure and dynamic of the creation, then *God* will be found at work at *every* level. God will be the name given to the thrust in the creation that provides initial aims for every occasion out of the vast continuum of possibility; he will be the lure that is active in all enticement towards fulfillment when the initial aim is accepted as subjective purpose; he will be the recipient of the good that is achieved in the world as such goals are reached and the total community of existents is enriched, while he will also be participant in the frustrations and disappointments that follow when wrong goals are chosen, limited results are obtained, and the total good is not promoted. Finally, he will use that which has thus been contributed by creaturely occasions; having taken those contributions into his "consequent nature" (Whitehead's term for God-as-affected-by-the-world) he can and does plough them back into the world in order to bring about more good in the process of creative advance.

Such a God can be no static substance. He cannot be so much the "exception to all metaphysical principles" required to explain how things go that he has but an external relationship, or a merely logical one, to the creation. He cannot be cause and in no sense effect. On the contrary, the give-and-take, the mutuality, the interpenetration and interrelationship we see in us and about us are also true of God. Here there is a sharp contrast with traditional ways of speaking about deity. In process thought God is stable in character, persistent in aim, unchangeable in his faithfulness; yet he is not above and beyond all becoming. He shares in becoming, enjoying enrichment, experiencing the world's anguish and its joy, surpassing himself in his earlier states, precisely because he is Love. He does not become *more* divine, *more* God, than he has been; and he is not surpassed or surpassable by anything not himself since he is the supremely excellent, all-righteous, all-good, all-loving One in relationship to each and every creaturely occasion. But *in* that relationship he is open to change in application and reference; his inexhaustible, indefatigable, and entirely adequate love works differently in different places to meet different circumstances. He expresses himself in various ways—shall we not say more at one time and place than at an other?—in a fashion appropriate to the opportunities offered to his love by the genuinely free decisions of the creatures.

This brings us to stress once more the reality of those creaturely decisions—and not only their reality but their highly significant place in the total pattern. God is indeed the chief causative agent in creation, providing inital aims, working through lures, in fact active in all creaturely events; but he is not the only cause. To be a cause, through decision at the appropriate level and in the appropriate manner, is inherent in every existing entity. The self-awareness of each of us indicates this. It would be meaningless for us to talk, as we so regularly and so naturally do, of the decisions we make as our *own,* with the conviction that they count seriously in what goes on, if there were not truth in this conviction of ours. We make decisions for which we feel ourselves responsible; we are sure that they are sufficiently important to have consequences. God, then, is not to be "blamed" for everything that happens as if he were the only responsible agent, and hence as if all creaturely activity were a mere irrelevance or at best the motions of a puppet whose strings are pulled by the divine producer of a marionette show. God is indeed able to "use" the less good in such a way that more good may emerge; in the biblical phrase, "he can make even the wrath of man turn to his praise." But this does not mean that he does everything that happens, either directly or indirectly. Above all, it does not mean that he does evil or wrong things that contradict his righteousness, goodness, and love. Nor is he so egotistical that he claims credit for all the good things that are done. He delights in seeing his creatures respond to his provision of aim and his action through lure, so that by their free decision they achieve good, while he also sorrows with them and suffers beside them—"the fellow-sufferer who understands", as Whitehead said—when the wrong is done and when things do not promote the true good that is within their reach.

Now let us see what this comes to in terms of our picture of human existence, bringing together the existentialist analysis and the process conceptuality. What does this tell us about ourselves as sinners?

The first point is simply to repeat that each of us is a living and dynamic personality in the making. The important thing about us is not the present moment in which we stand but the direction in which we are going. Each of us is a capacity for fulfillment, for the actualizing of the potentialities open to us for our responsible decision. No man or woman is a complete and finished entity. Both existentialism and process thought insist upon this view of human life as on the move towards the future. They tell us that every man and woman is continually using past experience as a way to realize future goals. Each of us is open to what is around us, taking from it that which seems to contribute to our coming to be; at the same time, each affects the environment with decisions that change the situation for better or for worse.

Next, each is possessed of what we have called an initial aim—a vocation, if you will, which he or she is to fulfill. That vocation is *to become human*, in the truest meaning of the word. We are to accept the aim and to use everything that is available for us to use so that the aim may be realized. This animating purpose, this vocation, is inalienably our own. Yet at the same time each is no "windowless monad", no isolated instance of individuality, but is open to others, lives with them, shares in the total human situation, and is unable even to continue significantly in existence without fellow men and women. We are also related in intimate societal terms with the total environment that is ours; we cannot be described, much less understood, unless we see that this is the case. Just as our past has its role in moulding us, so our present circumstances have their role. They play their necessary part in contributing to our becoming human. We are personalized parts of a total social process; we are in solidarity with our fellows and with the world. Our decisions, whatever they may be, contribute to and produce modifications in that total social process.

To say this is not to call in question the inalienable selfhood of each person. Our direction or routing is a linking of our own past, our own present, and our own future, however much there have been other pressures and influences upon us. Hence we must assume responsibility for what we are becoming and for the means we adopt towards effecting that becoming. This responsibility is for each decision; it is also towards the future. Our use of what affects us is the way we fulfill our human function; we cannot foist off that responsibility upon anyone else. Yet in our responsible decisions our aim plays its role too. The goals we have in view, the realization of the possibilities relevant to our decision, the contribution we will have made— or failed to make—enter into the picture. What we will to become is for us a clue to what we do here and now in the act of becoming.

As a personality in the making, along with one's fellows and in the world to which one belongs, each man and woman is capable of rational choice, able to act upon that choice, and responsible for what is done in willing the good that is before him or her. Each is also a *desire;* a mind, yes, and a will, yes, but a desire too. This desire is expressed in a yearning for the fulfillment possible for him or her. It involves also relationship with others. In the depths of selfhood he or she yearns to be united with them, to be at one with them in the mutuality we call love. Each wants to share, to give and to receive, to live with another and others. If a person experiences something of this love, he or she senses that the way to more adequate personal existence is being followed. If he or she rejects love, in the sense just described, there is a feeling of diminishment, with awareness of a failure to move forward into true unity of life, sinking back instead into a present that soon becomes a dead past that drags back, rather than a living past that urges on. Freedom in further decision is then less than it was; a man or woman is restricted more and more to selfish, unshared, acts that do not promote wider good and cannot even further his or her own best good. Here I can only appeal to my readers to look into themselves and see that what I have just been saying is the very truth they perceive there.

We have said that the Bible portrays human existence as a

body-mind or sense-spirit. So also do existentialist analysis and process thought. Our physical nature is included in what we are making of ourselves. Often enough we cannot even tell whether the body affects the spirit more than the spirit the body; but in fact both are always included in what we do. Just here human sexuality has its important place in human existence. Sexuality is the name we give to the total thrust of the whole person in the desire to be united with others. It is inclusive of that whole person, since both bodily equipment (which makes explicit sexual acts possible) and emotional response, as well as the identification of the mind with another mind and the will with another will, play a role. In another book, *Making Sexuality Human* (United Church Press, 1970), I have sought to discuss this at some length; suffice it now to say that any description of human existence that claims to be adequate must give a real place to this organic basis for love as we experience it, yearn for it, and seek to be fulfilled by it.

We owe a great deal to the depth psychologists for their work in this and related areas. We also owe much to them for their clinical description of human personality in the making, a description that remarkably parallels the existentialist analysis and fills out with vivid content the conceptuality of process thought. But perhaps their special contribution has been in opening up to us the hidden depths of human personality where the desires and drives of men and women work at a very profound level with inescapable consequences, bringing them to decide and to act in the ways in which they do. Yet insofar as some of these experts may suggest that an awareness of the "depths", which so seriously influence decision, shows that nobody is truly responsible for what is done, they are going far beyond the evidence and contradicting in theory what they are trying to establish in practice. They are denying what we know about ourselves. For no matter how much we are the creatures of unconscious influences, we still talk of ourselves and think of ourselves as those who can and who do choose. Further, it is to be observed that even the therapists who talk theoretically in this way and hence who minimize the reality of freedom and decision are themselves concerned in their practice to eradicate illicit influences on the self and to free their patients to choose and act responsibly. They want to get rid of secret repressions, concealed motivations, and the like, so that their patients may rise to the stature of true human life, making their choices as freely as possible and prepared to assume proper responsibility for the decisions they have made.

In respect to such matters, nobody is in the position to judge another. We cannot enter sufficiently into the other's past and present, nor discern the other's desires and the degree of freedom the other enjoyed at any given moment. Yet each of us recognizes in himself or herself personal obligation in matters of choice; and the person who is most conscious of failures and most keenly sensitive to pressures that have worked upon him or her will still be ready to say "I did choose this or that." The depth psychologist, whatever his or her theory may say, wishes to make just this affirmation a genuine experienced possibility.

Our special interest in this book is with the facts in human experience that led our ancestors to talk about sin. We have now begun to work towards the reconception of sin or human wrongness, since it is in the realm of free and responsible decision that this wrongness is located. But there is also the situation, the "state" in which each of us finds himself or herself before and at the time of making conscious decisions. In a later chapter we shall turn to that situation, speaking of human wrongness both as a state and as a series of acts. For the situational aspect of sin is closely related to the insight that each person is a social becoming, to which process thought in particular has drawn our attention. But first we should try to place sin or human wrongness in the context of the other evils, as we call them, that are present in the world-process in its larger sense. It is to that consideration that the next chapter will be devoted.

The relationship between what we have been saying in the present chapter and the discussion of biblical material in the preceding one ought to be obvious. I conclude by making a few remarks on this relationship. The language of the Bible and that of both existentialist analysis and process thought are very different. Yet in all of them, human life is seen as dynamic and changing. In all of them there is an emphasis on becoming. In all of them there is an insistence on responsibility. There is also a stress on social relationships and the way in which these have their effect, since we influence others quite as much as they influence us. Furthermore, there is the recognition of the power of love and it is seen that we are indeed made "for love", without which we are less than we might be and should be. In all of them there is the understanding that we are being made for cooperation, as "fellow-workers" (in biblical idiom) or as "co-creators" (in process language) with the drive for good that moves through the creation. And there is insistence that the proper fulfillment of human subjective aim or purpose is in becoming a personality in close communion or fellowship with others, which means that we find ourselves most truly when each is the personal, or personalized, agent for a Love that is cosmic in sweep and unfailing in operation—the Love that seeks always to bring about more created love, in righteousness and goodness.

That cosmic Love is called by the religious person, once delivered from immature or idolatrous models of deity, by the ancient and hallowed word "God." Both biblical thought and modern existentialist and process thinking recognize that human failure, distortion, or violation of right relationship, which is his basic wrongness, is a refusal, small or great, of human destiny in its noblest reach: to become a child, a son or daughter of God, a created lover who reflects the cosmic Lover, and acts for him in thought and word and deed.

4
"Sin" in the Context
of a Processive World View

In many discussions of human wrongness, it is regarded as
but one instance of the more general "problem of evil", as it is
called. We are told that there are various sorts of evil in the
world: natural evil, meaning such things as tidal waves, earth-
quakes, and volcanic eruptions; animal evil, in which reference
is made to the cruelty seen in animate life below the human
level, where one beast is killed by another and where parasites
live on (and eventually destroy) their "host"; physical and
mental evil, or human suffering due to disease and accident, as
well as the distressing senility of the aged and the anguish often
experienced by the dying; and finally moral evil or human
wrongness, including "the inhumanity of man to man", disobedience to the "moral law", and enmity against God. In a
world in which religious people believe they see the presence
and activity of a good or loving God, how can we explain these
aspects of evil?

There is some justification for bringing all these together
under the category of evil, in that each instance seems to us to be
an unnecessary and distressing disordering of the world. On the
other hand, it is my belief that the dumping of all these in one
heap, so to say, has led to much confusion of thought. Furthermore, it rests upon a certain inaccuracy of description. We shall
turn to this matter in a moment. In any event, I should say,
human wrongness or sin (as the biblical writers intend the word,
anyway) is different from other evils, even from moral evil as
this is commonly understood by philosophical writers on the
subject. Human wrongness is both more tragic than other evils

and also more susceptible of understanding, provided we recognize the high degree of consciously exercised freedom at the human level of creation.

But let us first speak of what appear to be necessary distinctions or discriminations among the various aspects of the world that are commonly described as evil. For example, it is surely odd to think that an earthquake is evil. When it happens, as it does from time to time in certain places on the planet, it is primarily a natural readjustment of the stuff of which the physical world is made, caused (as we are told) by the repatterning that is inevitable on a planet burning hot in the centre, cooler on the periphery, and continually contracting. Only when human beings and perhaps other animate creatures are present in the earthquake area and suffer from the fact could we speak meaningfully of evil's taking place. For then we have what a friend of mine has styled "a head-on collision between natural coercive force and persons who have the capacity to feel and think." Similarly with tidal waves, the result of a readjustment of the ocean bed; with hurricanes, which have a meteorological cause; and with volcanic eruptions, with their release of energy pent up in the earth and inexorably seeking and finding release. To describe all these as evil *sans phrase* is a mistake.

In respect to evil in the animal realm, we are indeed confronted by what can seem the terrifying spectacle of "nature red in tooth and claw." Yet we are told by zoologists and biologists that the actual pain suffered in animal killing, to take but one instance, is much less than it appears to us. When we see a crab tear off the claw of another crab, not for sustenance but apparently in sheer delight, we should not read either our human feeling of anger nor our human sense of pain into the incident. An acquaintance who is expert in this field tells me that the pain is probably little more than a momentary and severe twinge. This seems to minimize matters too much. But I believe that we often commit the pathetic fallacy here by assuming that the suffering is identical with what ours would be if an arm were torn from our body. Nor do animals kill in anger, but usually only when threatened or in need of food. Surely there is not the intentional cruelty we see so frequently in human infliction of suffering.

In physical and mental suffering among people, we must recognize that the physiological equipment that makes anguish possible also makes pleasure possible. The conditions for one are the conditions for the other. So also in mental suffering. This is probably much more terrible than actual physical pain, but we need to see that the psychological factors that serve to produce anguish also serve to provide happiness, while fellow-suffering with another person is based upon the same community of feeling that can bring companionship in joy.

But I shall not pursue this matter further. I hope that it is plain that I do not intend to minimize the suffering in the world, nor to deny that there are real evils confronting us. At the same time I think that we can find, in all honesty, certain "meliorizing" considerations that somewhat relieve the picture. I have discussed this in my previously mentioned book *Goodness Distorted*. Here I wish only to say that human wrongness, as I have called it, has its context in a world where evil does occur, yet that it is to be carefully distinguished from evil in the more general sense in which we usually use the word. It is my belief that a processive view of the world gives us considerable help both in understanding the origin of evil in that more general sense and in coming to terms with the tragic facts of human existence in wrongness to which the word "sin" has always pointed. A processive view does not explain away either evil or human wrongness; it provides, however, a context in which they may be interpreted—and that, I take it, is a useful contribution to our thinking.

This *is* a world in process, as I have so often urged. It is not a completed world, in which everything is now entirely *done*. Christian theology ought not to speak of creation only in the past tense, saying that God *created* the world. Rather, it ought to speak of the world *as being created*. In one of his poems the Catholic writer Alfred Noyes put it in the right way: "Now and forever God makes earth and heaven. . . ." So the world is a continuous "coming into existence", a creative becoming. Once that is recognized, we can also recognize that we are in no position to stand off and judge this or that particular momentary "point of arrival" as if nothing more were to come afterwards. To use a hackneyed illustration, nobody would think of judging a carpenter's shop or the work of the carpenter by the sawdust, the chips of wood, or the unpolished and incomplete state of the table being made by the craftsman. The illustration fails us since it suggests an external workman, who is not "in" his product; yet it makes a necessary point in respect to the incompleteness of the world. Things are "in the making"; they must be seen in that way and appraised in terms of the end in view, rather than of this or that moment along the line.

In the general creative advance the determining purpose is the bringing into existence of new entities, occasions, or energy-events, which through their realization of the good possible for them can express, in increasing adequacy, the cosmic Love that urgently desires to share itself. Thomas Aquinas, with other traditional theologians, saw this when he spoke of *bonum diffusivum sui*—genuine good that by its very nature must "spread itself." Goodness cannot be self-contained or it ceases to be good. Precisely because God's character, his very nature and "stuff", is sheer love, it must extend itself and seek more and more opportunities for its activity. Love-in-action as God's "nature and his agency in the world" (as Whitehead once put it) gives itself to others, endeavouring always to bring to fruition the possibilities available to each and every occasion in the creation. How is this accomplished?

The Christian answers this question, phrased in such processive terms, by saying that the supreme Love, God himself, brings into existence a certain patterning in creation where it is possible for his love to lure the creaturely events to their truest fulfillment. But even before Christian faith emerged, the Greek philosopher Plato glimpsed this answer. In the *Timaeus* Plato says that the *demiourgos* or "divine craftsman" is himself entirely good; and because he is good, he wishes to share his goodness with others. Therefore he fashions a world in which that goodness may be given concrete expression. He delights in making this possible and in giving a share in his perfection to other entities, and he does this by persuasive means rather than by "forcing" goodness upon those others. Indeed it is impossible to force goodness upon anything, since the very nature of goodness requires that it be freely accepted and freely expressed.

The myth in which Plato tells about the creation of the world is not acceptable as it stands, of course; but it is "a likely tale", to use his own words about myths, and the insight that inspires it is both profound and helpful. In his urgent desire to share his goodness, Plato says, the *demiourgos* contemplates the "forms" or the possibilities that are eternally available; he strives to impress these upon the material stuff with which he must work if anything at all is to come into existence. Exactly how we understand this material stuff, this *anangke* or primordial necessity, will depend upon other considerations. In the process conceptuality we should say that it is a "creativity" that is basic to everything, both divine and creaturely. In any event, it is clear that for Plato God never "exists" entirely alone, even in a supposed period "before creation." What he intends to tell us is that the *demiourgos* is always creative and that to think of him is at the same time to think of a created world in which he works for the emergence of participated goodness.

Christian theologians have usually rejected this idea because to their mind it seems to infringe upon the "absolute" nature of God. But there may very well be ways in which the Platonic conception can be stated that do not deny the supremacy and perfection of God, although the introduction of the ambiguous term "absolute" must be avoided since it introduces into the picture ideas of a *kind* of perfection or supremacy that usually entails immutability and a static excellence. Here a suggestion by a distinguished contemporary theologian seems to me both interesting and useful.

In *The Christian Faith* (Hodder and Stoughton, 1964), Dr. F. W. Dillistone says: "It is possible to suggest that the word 'create' as used by the Bible was an artistic rather than a scientific word, and that its use by scientists has not served the interests of clarification. If, however, the precise scientific reference is omitted, it then becomes possible to imagine the universe as a meaningful whole and as the work of a personal mind shaping available materials. Whence the materials come, the Bible does not enquire. That a formless concentration of energy might have existed with God before the creation of the world does not seem to me an impossible conception to entertain."

Following this line of thought, we might say that God works with a "formless concentration of energy" and from it brings into existence new and significant occasions through which his creative purpose may be expressed. It would certainly be better to say that this exists not *before* creation (since that would imply a time when God as creator did not "have" a creation, a notion that to some of us is absurd) but as ceaselessly providing for him, at all times and places, the continuing material with which he is working as he acts to bring into existence the occasions in which his goodness or love may be expressed. We know nothing at all of a *before* or *after* creation, in any literal temporal sense of the words; we know only the creation as it now presents itself to us and in which we live. By faith we also know of the cosmic Love that works creatively in the world. The talk of *before* and *after* is mythological; it is concerned to say something about what God is always up to, in himself and in respect to his purpose for the world, as well as in the realization of that purpose through the creation of which we are a part.

As so often, reading the Bible as if it were a scientific manual or a literal historical record can lead us astray. Certainly the Genesis story is what in the second chapter we have said it is: a mythological way of affirming God's boundless creativity, his utter supremacy, and the dependence of all things upon his creative action. Read in that fashion, the Genesis story does not contradict the point Dr. Dillistone was making. Even Aquinas, we may recall, found nothing intrinsically wrong in the notion that God eternally creates the world. It was only because he believed, as did everyone in his age, that the creation story in Genesis must be taken in a literal historical sense that he felt obliged to call this concept of an eternal creation (everlasting would be better word here) into question. Since we do not take the Genesis material in that literal sense, we have no reason to reject the view that God *and* the world are always there, and there together, although we must be clear that the world in its present patterning is dependent upon God for the goods that are being accomplished in it.

Creation need not mean that first there was quite literally nothing and then (a split second later) there was a world. Even the doctrine that God creates *ex nihilo* ("out of nothing") need not be interpreted in that wooden and simple-minded way. It can mean that, from among the range of possibilities and by the use of the materials antecedent events have already moulded, God brings into existence something that is genuinely new as a specific emergent event that yet is in continuity with what has gone before and with the total process of creative advance. The genuinely new is a configuration, a constellation, a focusing, an entity with its own initial aim, its own potentialities, its own capacity for decision, its own opportunity to actualize and hence bring to fulfillment what God purposes—but with opportunity also, by the same capacity for decision, to fail to do this. The word "nothing" in this context need not signify some hypothetical absolute *nihil* but simply the absence of that particular actualized occasion from the world hitherto.

In what we know of creation and in our own experience of personality in the making, we see a process in which such "inherited" configurations are modified so that novelty appears. This process is not automatic; neither is it dictated from on high. Influences and pressures have their part to play, both from the past and in the present, both material and mental or spiritual. But the major *creaturely* factor is the decision made by the particular occasion. This decision need not be highly conscious; we have already indicated that at certain levels it cannot be such, at least in the sense that we humans would give to the word "consciousness." But there is always decision, in that certain specific and relevant possibilities for routing or direction are accepted and other such possibilities are rejected. In choosing *this,* we "cut off" *that.* Thus each energy-event—I trust that by now it will be seen that I use, for the sake of variety, the terms "occasion", "occurrence", "event", "entity", and "energy-event" synonymously, even if this is a not quite accurate usage—is in a very genuine sense *causa sui*; it causes or creates itself. To deny this is to deny our own personal awareness of what it means to "become." Yet to say this does not imply that God has no part in the process nor suggest that there is no circumambient reality that lures us towards the right choice. It tells us, however, that God does not coerce us into this or that specific choice. God lets us "make ourselves", so to say, although in the making his purpose is at stake; and he is also able to use even wrong decisions in a way that ultimately can produce good results. For the Christian, the crucifixion of Jesus is the supreme instance of God's doing just this. We are free to accept the lure or to reject it. We can prehend positively or negatively among the influences pouring upon us. We are able to say yes or we may choose to say no. And whatever choice we make, there are bound to be consequences.

The consequences are for our own good or ill. But they do not stop with us, with our own particular human existence as personalities in the making. In a process that is social in nature and in which our human existence is in solidarity with our fellows, the choices we make have consequences that affect others and ultimately affect the social situation as a whole. At every level in the creative process, although perhaps in less obvious ways, the same is true. Decisions have a determinative result in how the creative advance will go on, whether it will be towards the fullest satisfaction of each entity, whether it will be diverted onto another path, whether it will be stopped here or there so that right advance is prevented. And in a broader sense decisions have a determinative result on the *total* creative movement, since these decisions are made by the energy-events of which that advance is composed and can move it forward along the line of ever-fuller realization of good, or can distort and frustrate it.

One thinks of a river that is flowing towards the sea. For the most part, perhaps, it moves on steadily and majestically. But there are backwaters, side streams, and diversions that have no outlet back into the mainstream. The mainstream continues on its way; but the backwaters reduce its volume, the side streams go off in different directions and only after some considerable distance manage to rejoin the mainstream; and the diversions, lacking any outlet, become stagnant since there is no way in which the water can get out of its confining limits. The analogy is very imperfect, to be sure, but it has its usefulness. For one thing, it shows something of the ongoing of the universe despite the failures and impediments that occur in it. It rules out the notion of a merely automatic advance, because it allows for such failures and impediments. But it makes clear that there *is* a main line of advance, a sound and healthy direction; and when that line is followed, the advance goes forward towards its intended goal.

Because there is the capacity to decide (as an inalienable characteristic of entities or occasions at every level), there is always the chance that from the continuum of possibility any particular occasion will select a lesser rather than a greater good. Why this happens in the given instance we cannot say; if we could say why, in the sense of providing a full explanation, freedom of decision would effectively be denied. Freedom, to be *genuine* freedom, must be self-posited, explicable by nothing other than itself. It is of course true that when we look back, we can think of what we call "reasons" or "causes" for this or that choice; but this is possible for us because we *are* looking back rather than actually engaged in the act of deciding. The factors that have entered into the decision then appear to us, when we look back, to have been determinative; yet when we were in the moment of choice we were quite aware of our ability to say yes or no within the limits provided by time and place and circumstance.

While no full explanation is possible, however, we may make some suggestions of a very general sort that will be helpful in our thinking. Confronted by a variety of possible choices, among which we must decide, there will be some or perhaps only one that can be styled obviously attractive, apparently satisfying, or immediately available. There will be one or more others less readily "at hand", less obviously pleasing, less plainly able to provide us with an immediate sense of satisfaction. Each of us knows this well enough, once he looks at those decisive moments, however minor some of them may seem.

A student has an examination tomorrow morning; the grade he will receive will be crucial for his future success. But a friend invites him to go to see a film that has been highly praised by the critics and that will doubtless be entertaining, maybe even instructive. Is the student to decide to spend the evening in preparation for the examination, or is he to go to the theatre where the film is being shown? Most of us would say that the former choice would be better and wiser and in the long run much more rewarding. Yet most of us would also admit that the latter choice is easier to make, for it promises an evening of entertainment in company with a friend, which in its own fashion promises also to be rewarding. Which choice will the student make? His seriousness of purpose, his rational understanding, and his desire to be a success in his future profession will impel him in one direction. His delight in his friend's companionship, his desire for an evening's relaxation, even some degree of reasonable thinking, will impel him in the other. Nonetheless, decide he must; and he is free to say yes or no—again within the limits of time, place, and circumstance.

This is by no means an unusual or infrequent situation in human existence. Indeed, it is a typical and inevitable one. Decisions must be made. The temptation is to make them without much ado, on the basis of what at the given moment is appealing, available, pleasant. Nor can the decisions be "unmade" and their consequences avoided. This is how the backwaters, side streams, and dead ends come to be. This is what genuine evil is all about. It is not a radical corruption of the stuff of creation; neither is it chosen because it is *known* to be wrong. Nobody chooses evil save "under the aspect of good", as the moral theologians of the Christian tradition have insistently reminded us. Nothing is *malum in se,* in and of itself wrong. But the good that is *not* the proper good at *that* time and in *that* place and for *those* ends (whatever all these may be) is nothing other than an *empirical evil.* It is fraudulent in its appeal, although in and of itself it is not positively evil. Indeed, in one sense it is a negation of a greater possible good, although this need not bring us to subscribe to the platonizing view of some early Christian thinkers who said that all evil is either privation or negation and has no positive "quality" about it. The sense in which it *is* negation is that it prevents the realization of the good that would have been more rewarding and would have contributed more adequately to the ongoing creative advance for all concerned.

Responsibility rests here with the agent who makes the decisions. It is a grave error to make God responsible for decisions that are made by the creaturely agent, when it is apparent that these decisions often render the purposes of God less effective or actually hinder their fulfillment. Equally it is an error to say that every right decision, for the greater good, is not really made by the agent but by God. And at the human level it is *not* true, in any obvious sense, that "every virtue we possess, and every victory won, and every thought of holiness, are his [God's] alone", even if a hymn does state this. The fact is that the world is being created in a fashion that makes human choices *count,* either for good or for ill. We are responsible for them; and in this way our choices help or hinder the advancement of the divine purpose in the world.

How then does God come into the picture? The answer is to be found by recalling what has been said earlier in this book. God provides the initial aim that makes for the genuine fulfillment of each occasion. God surrounds each with his care, providing a lure through creaturely entities towards that fulfillment. God makes sure that fulfillment will in fact be the result of a freely chosen movement towards the subjective aim or goal; he guarantees that such fulfillment will give genuine satisfaction. God receives into his "consequent nature" the good that has been achieved, perhaps even the agent who has done the achieving (this may be what "resurrection" signifies), while the evil that remains is a surd. Yet even then the evil is for God an opportunity for a different but nonetheless real good. God ploughs back into the world the positive accomplishments in creation he has received, enjoyed, and can use, so that greater good will be known in more places and in more ways. God acts in love, for love, by love, and through love; since he *is* Love cosmic and supreme and perfect.

Because God is Love he cannot use coercion save in those very restricted areas of subhuman and human existence where only in this way can he prevent inevitable contrast from producing sheer chaos, and thus avert the threat of a world completely out of hand. Perhaps this is what "the wrath of God" really means. But wherever force is exercised by God, it is minimal and is in the hands of the cosmic Lover, in whose service it is not sheer or mere power but essentially the strength of love exerted by One who knows what he is doing and "restrains" himself in that doing according to his basic quality of loving mercy. However this may be—and some process theologians would feel that here I have conceded too much by allowing *any* use of force— God will not and cannot coerce free and responsible agents to do that which in his wisdom he knows is for their best good. Yet he has sufficient resources of love to overcome evil in the world and wrongness in humankind to "save" us from our sin, as we commonly put it, and to make "all things work together towards a good end." Certainly this is an affirmation of Christian faith and can be known only through some meeting with the divine Love. It does not entail divine interference in the world, as from outside; it means persuasive and concerned work, from within, as the agents are lured to make free and responsible decisions that will bring to them the fullness of life they *really* desire, even if they are not keenly aware of it, and that God purposes for them.

The wrongness of human existence, our sin, must be set in just such a general view of the world. Thus sin, in the first instance, is a matter of choice, made in all freedom and with full responsibility. It is a refusal to follow the sound and right direction of advance, rather than some supposedly radical perversion of the stuff of creation. It is a failure to advance when advance is desirable. It is self-seeking in its most unhappy form, with a disregard of others and of God. It is inexcusable and contagious. It is a willingness to go off on some side path, to rest content in a backwater, to refuse to respond to a lure towards good. In a word, it is wilful nonfulfillment of potentiality, a settling for modes of satisfaction that are not in the best interests of each and of all. And it is tragic, horrible, and frightening.

Since the creative process is in and under the divine Lover who seeks always the best possible fulfillment, sin results in alienation from his purpose and estrangement from the goal he proposes. Furthermore, because the divine Lover is always in intimate relationship with the creation, and because cooperation with his ongoing purpose is for the creature its one way of being rightly related to him, the decisions violating that purpose are also a violation of the intentional relationship of the agent with God himself. Thus everything that we have found pointed to by the term "sin" is included in this revised view. When it comes to the human situation as a whole with the solidarity of the individual with society, with the fact that decisions have consequences and that these are in commonalty shared, and that for good or ill this sharing affects the general condition of mankind in its solidarity, we can see that once again this represents another way of stating the reality with which traditional theology was dealing when it spoke of humanity's "sinful state" or "original sin." The tragic and serious situation the human race has created for itself through long accumulation of wrong decisions and wilful choice is not to be denied; it is to be affirmed, but in a different way.

I had almost said, "the situation into which the human race has fallen", but I avoided that way of phrasing it because of the danger that the introduction of the word "fall" might suggest that the old picture of "original righteousness" from which we "fell" into "original sin" could still be taken literally and presented as valid for us today. I do not think this is the case. But I believe that we can continue to use the older words if only we interpret "original righteousness" as the divine purpose or intention for continued human fulfillment through choices contributing to the common good; and interpret "original sin" as that concrete present situation to which our human solidarity has brought us—in fact to the place where the selection of the true good is extraordinarily difficult, although not entirely impossible, and where there is a continuing tendency (called in classical theology "concupiscence") to select the worse rather than the better way towards self-realization.

On the whole, however, I incline to think that it is better no longer to use these traditional terms. Their associations are often misleading when not actually mistaken. I quite realize that to some this frank statement of opinion will only confirm them in their feeling that what I have been saying is remote not only from traditional theology but also from what they take to be biblical teaching. Yet I am convinced that the *sense* of both is in fact preserved, although the language is vastly different. As I have said so frequently, we should not let ourselves be enamoured of words, which are always relative to particular circumstances and may with time become very unfortunate and misleading. If the *sense* is preserved, as in my judgement it is here, we may use whatever words seem appropriate. When we are too meticulous about the retention of the traditional words, we may find ourselves in the odd position of conveying to other people meanings entirely different from, perhaps even opposite to, those that were first intended by the words themselves.

Some may feel that this effort at interpretation is altogether mistaken. Such critics will include the so-called "fundamentalists" who simply cannot accept the idea that the Bible may be used in the way we have done and who reject the notion that the world is a creative process rather than a "finished article." Very few thoughtful people accept that position nowadays, however. There are also some who will not grant the epigenetic concept of evolution but retain the 19th-century view that there is nothing more in the world than a mechanical reshuffling of bits of matter. These critics are the exact opposite of the fundamentalists; it is their contention that the interpretative enterprise is mistaken because there is nothing worth interpreting. For them the entire Christian position is false and we should give it up altogether. There are also those who find so patent a contradiction between the kind of interpretation we have suggested and what they take to be the biblical and conventional theological teaching (which last two they tend to confuse) that they prefer to compartmentalize their thinking. They wish to keep their theology in one box and their world view, scientifically and philosophically speaking, in another. This position seems to me impossible; and the great merit of men like Teilhard de Chardin and Whitehead is that they saw the absurdity of such compartmentalizing and insisted that theology and everything else must be brought into a close relationship.

I conclude this chapter with a brief summary of its main

points. The world must be understood as a process and not as a completed product. In such a process, the important consideration is the direction that is being taken, either towards, or away from, the true fulfillment of each energy-event. This fulfillment is the realization by each actual entity of its subjective aim, through accepting the initial aim provided for it and through relevant decisions, among those available for its choice, by selecting that which makes for the greatest common good. The end that is ultimately sought is goodness shared as widely as possible; and this signifies participation in the love that is God's own nature, his mode of activity, and his goal. To cooperate with God is to be a co-creator and fellow-worker with him, following the right and true line or direction towards the fulfillment that is his purpose. Yet each entity is free to elect otherwise, preferring to follow a path that is not in accordance with the divine purpose of righteousness, goodness, and love. It can say 'no' to its intended goal of satisfaction in love. When it makes such a decision, it retards the creative movement, it diverts energies into side streams, and it can even reject all advance and try to remain where it is, in self-satisfied contentment in its decision. Evil is the name we may give to these failures and refusals, whether consciously made or made without such vivid awareness.

Since the process is social in nature, decisions made by any one entity inevitably affect and influence every other entity. Thus the process as a whole, moving forward along the line of creative advance, includes elements within it that are like surds; they do not work towards the actualizing of its proper ends. At the level of human existence in particular, where conscious and responsible decisions are to be made, this is caused by refusal to grasp the relevant possibilities; or more tragically it is the result of wilful decision for some specious or inadequate good whose appeal and attraction are obvious but whose ability to give what they seem to offer is sadly deficient. In the mode of togetherness that is specifically human, such choices not only damage the movement towards authentic self-realization of each person but also have enormously serious consequences for the human community as a whole, both in the present and in the future.

This is the tragedy of our human situation in its alienation and estrangement, where men and women do not choose their authentic selfhood, where they are separated from their fellows, and where they violate their proper relationship with God.

Sin is a matter of human decisions for goods that are inadequate or unsatisfying; it is a serious and damaging impeding of the movement towards personality. It is also a matter of the social consequences of such decisions, resulting in a situation that makes it difficult—well-nigh impossible—to decide rightly and then act upon such right decisions. Because we all share in that situation, we suffer alienation from the purpose of God and estrangement from others. Thus there is a schism in the inner existence of the persons who form the human community, a breaking of the wholesome relationship all are intended to have with the cosmic Love. In the following chapter we shall consider in more detail that human situation or "state" into which we are born, as well as say something more about the concrete decisions for wrong that we make as responsible and free creative agents.

5
"Sin" as a State

The frequent use of the word "situation" in earlier chapters will have indicated that I prefer that term to "state", which is used in the title of this chapter. But "state" is the traditional term so I have employed it here. On the other hand, the way in which this human state must be described, from the perspective we are taking in this study, is different from what is said in most "accepted" theology; although I repeat that the facts of the case—the human race in its alienation and estrangement, in its breaking of the intended relationship of men and women with God and with one another—must be accepted by anybody who can observe and reflect.

I have stressed the social solidarity of the human race, the way in which all of us are participant one with others in the social process that is going on at the human level. Ours is a world in which whatever happens to any one occasion affects all other occasions. There is no such thing as an entirely isolated and insulated individual. This solidarity, which is true generally and throughout the creation, is true *a fortiori* on the specifically human level. Yet we have stressed that this mutual relationship does not deny nor reduce the freedom that is proper to each entity as it makes the decisions open to it from among the relevant possibilities that present themselves; neither does it diminish the responsibility of each entity for the particular decisions it makes. Of course there are limits to freedom, set by place where, time when, and conditions under which it finds itself; of course there is a limit to responsibility where freedom is less than complete. Nonetheless, the reality of freedom and of responsibility remains; in our moments of self-awareness we all recognize this and in our moments of decision we act upon it.

Now by divine intention and the divine purpose of right-

eousness, goodness, and love, the human situation is meant to
be marked by the mutuality in which each works with and for his
and her fellows as "the servant of others", and in so acting also
finds fulfillment. "Each for all and all for each", as the old
saying goes, is the divinely intended state of affairs. This intention, as I suggested in the last chapter, is what the term "original
righteousness", if it is retained at all, can be taken to signify.
The point is not that once upon a time, in the history of the race,
men and women lived in perfect relationship one with others and
in obedience to the divine Lover. We have no evidence for
anything of the sort. The idyllic picture in Genesis, portraying
humans in the Garden of Eden before "the Fall", is not factual
history; it is a mythological presentation of the human situation
as it is in the divine intention. It is also the situation towards
which the creative process, so far as we are concerned, is
directing itself; this is where things are going, *if* they go in the
right way.

Whether that blessed state will ever be realized in this
world of ours and on the level of human history in the future is a
subject for debate. But the Kingdom of God, for that is what the
picture really portrays, is nonetheless even now a present
reality in two senses. In the first place, it is everlastingly true in
God himself. In his "consequent nature" (as affected by the
creation) he receives, harmonizes, moulds, and enjoys all the
good that has been achieved in the world. His superabundant
love, thus realized, *is* his sovereign reign. But it is also, and in
the second place, true insofar as through response to the lure
that moves us there is a presence and action of God's loving
concern, his indefatigable care for the creation, in its every nook
and cranny—"every hair of your head is numbered", said Jesus, putting this in his own inimitable and picturesque way.
Here is no action "from without", nor a remote ideal offered to
the world; it is the immediacy of the divine presence and activity
in the here and now of the world's existence. In God the kingdom of love is always realized; the lure of his love is no mental
idea nor an interesting concept, but is God's actual working. For
nothing could be *more* real or factual than God himself, whether
in his "primordial nature" as inclusive of the continuum of

possibility, or in his "consequent nature" as recipient of the accomplishments of the creation by his positive prehension or acceptance *or* by his negative prehension or rejection. He uses everything usable that occurs both for the enjoyment that is his and also for further employment in establishing his righteousness, goodness, and love in the future.

The serious and tragic aspect of the human situation, however, is that the Kingdom of God, the sovereign rule of love in its fullness, is *not* in fact realized in the world as it might be, should be, and could be. The lure is there, to be sure; that is God's present activity. But the fulfillment of all good and loving possibilities does not take place in the situation we know and in which we live. We do not dwell together in perfect understanding; we do not all aid our fellows; we are not in the divinely intended relationship with him who is the divine Lover. On the contrary, through the inheritance received from past decisions for worse rather than better ends, the human situation is characterized by alienation and estrangement. It is this we may describe, if we again wish to use traditional language, by the phrase "original sin."

In that situation, with its alienation and estrangement, there is the tendency or urge to make the less worthy and less satisfying decisions. Those whose lives are lived by the necessity of their being human in the community of their fellows are not able to recognize, in each and every instance of decision, the better possibility and therefore to reject or dismiss the worse. What is more, the will to persist in efforts after the better is weakened by previous choices, so that the condition becomes ever more serious. The attraction of the immediately available and obviously present choice is so great that it requires a very considerable struggle to reject it and to elect the opposite possibility. What we and others have made of ourselves in the past must inevitably influence what we decide in the present. There is a self-determination here that cannot be evaded; we must reckon with this and realize that nobody makes choices *now* as if he or she had never made choices before—or as if he or she were not in the situation where other people's choices influence each one, whether those choices have been made in the near or remote past or whether they are now being made in the present.

We turn to a consideration of alienation and estrangement as these characterize the human situation. A first approach may be made by remembering a word often used by Pierre Teilhard de Chardin: "diminishment." Teilhard intended by this word to point to a reduction in human possibility as the capacity for acceptance of true good is lessened. This, he believed, is how things are, once wrongness is allowed to run its course. The consequence is a diminishment of each person's existence, through his or her own and through others' choices and actions. And it is precisely here that we find the manifestation of human alienation and estrangement.

We have said that any occasion or event is a focusing at one point of the past, the present, and the future. What has gone on in the past is "remembered", not only in conscious recollection but in the deepest reaches of the existence of each entity. The affects of the past are felt in the present and to greater or lesser degree determine the range of possible decisions at any given moment. In the *present* moment, the relationships in which the entity exists and by which it is inevitably influenced make their own contribution and again to greater or lesser degree determine the range of possibilities open for decision. Whether there is, or is not, a strictly contemporaneous participation of one event in another or whether some brief time-interval may be required, the fact of such influence is apparent. And the future thrust of the occasion, making its decisions towards or away from proper fulfillment of aim, is even more obvious in this determination. The identity of any series of occasions is established by its being a specific routing in which past, present, and future are brought together. Each new moment will modify, alter, change, add or subtract new features or old ones; yet the main line of advance, from past through present to future, makes it possible for us to speak meaningfully of this or that particular instance of routing or direction.

So likewise in the human situation. What has taken place in the *past* has its consequences in the present; the interrelationships known in the *now* are effectively influential; and the *future* aim towards which the thrust is made, with whatever adequacy or inadequacy, must play its significant part. What does this or that particular community strive for or aim at? What is the goal towards which men and women in their total community life are working? Because of the solidarity of the race, with each and every man or woman a participant in it, the human situation is a complex of the race's past, present, and future. The decisions made in the past are carried over into the present through their consequences; the immediate relationships of the present are inescapable in their effectual power; and future aims, be they for good or be they marked by refusal and deviation and failure on the part of the agents, inevitably modify the situation at any given moment. This totality is what we must have in mind when we try to analyze the condition in which each of us finds himself or herself.

Here, then, we have the background for the human sense of alienation. The word itself tells us that people know themselves to be at odds with their environment. But that is not all; they are at odds with themselves too, with their fellows, and with the divine purpose that is God's activity. And with alienation there comes estrangement. This estrangement is expressed in the sense of human failure, in the absence of possible and desirable relationships, and in an awareness of enmity against the grain of the universe or how things are meant to go. Against what or whom is this felt, deep down in our human existence?

In *The Courage to Be* Paul Tillich suggested that there are three aspects of alienation or estrangement that demand attention. Since his discussion of these is pertinent to our subject here, I venture to use his suggestions for our own particular purposes in this book. First, we feel ourselves alienated and estranged *from ourselves*. There is a rift in human selfhood of which we are conscious. Second, we feel ourselves alienated and estranged *from our neighbours*, our human brethen. The "unplumbed, salt, estranging sea" (in Matthew Arnold's phrase) separates us from those with whom we would be most intimately at one; each of us is their "enemy", although each wants to be their friend and comrade. Third, we feel ourselves alienated *from God* and estranged from that ultimate and supreme reality upon whom we depend for existence. We may not articulate this feeling by using words like "God"; nonetheless, the *meaning* of existence seems lost and each of us has the feeling that he or she is "a stranger and afraid / in a world he never made." To Tillich's three aspects I should wish to add a fourth. We feel ourselves alienated and estranged *from the creativity of the natural order*—from the actual world that is our environment. That world now seems to threaten us; we are not at home there; the creative process appears careless of us and we find ourselves continually drawn to fight against it rather than work with it.

Now if we take these four together we recognize that they are all ways of asserting that we are in a situation where we do not integrate our existence by centring it in that which is deepest, highest, most real both in ourselves and in creation. Hence we are disoriented. We feel this profoundly in moments of "quiet desperation", as Thoreau put it; or we have a pervasive if vague feeling of dis-ease that disturbs us and prevents our full enjoyment of life. In ourselves we are aware of some strange split; from the side of others, we see a dangerous attack on our own selfhood. In relationship with God or whatever we may call the supreme and ultimate reality or dynamic in the world, we are conscious of disobedience and a refusal on our part to respond. We look upon the creative natural process as something in which we have no real part and place.

For men and women who honestly look at themselves, "the times are out of joint." They do not fit in with how things go, and they do not belong as they might and should to the creative advance of which (without possibility of evasion) they are a part and to which they are entirely organic. Sensitive people, who have the ability to speak for all of us as we really are, know discontent, maladjustment, sometimes even appalling anguish.

Obviously, as I have just intimated, most of us most of the time do not have this four-fold sense of alienation and estrangement in the forefront of our thinking. From day to day we "get along", as the saying has it, to the best of our ability and we find our moments of happiness and delight. Yet there are those odd occasions, those times of "quiet desperation" (to repeat Thoreau's phrase), when we recognize that this *is* how things go with us. Any portrayal of human existence that does not include these moments in its purview is convicted of cheapness and superficiality. The experience of the race, as exemplified in the great tragedians, the poets, the artists, and the novelists, demonstrates the plain fact of a pervasive sense of failure, of absence, of diminishment. We must find place for it in whatever account we give of ourselves and of our human condition. It is just here that the existentialist analysis speaks so convincingly and compellingly to us, for the existentialists have been among those contemporary thinkers, continuous with many in the past, who have both seen this truth and bravely stated it for the rest of us.

This awareness of estrangement and alienation has given rise to the pessimistic philosophies and theologies that speak of "radical evil" in the world and above all in people, that talk of humanity as *massa perditionis* ("a lump of corruption", in St. Augustine's graphic phrase), or that regard the entire human story from beginning to end as nothing but "a tale told by an idiot, full of sound and fury, signifying nothing." But this extreme negative position will not do either. For Christians, at any rate, such a denigration of the world and human beings is equivalent to a denigration of God; and Christians must remember that our faith tells us that the world at heart is *good* because the chief causative agent in creation is good. In Genesis we read that as God "created" each bit of the world, he saw "that it was good"; of the whole enterprise, he saw that it was "very good" as it reached final expression in the appearance of humankind. And common sense also rejects any totally negative evaluation. Men and women do not live as if such were true. They know there is evil and wrong, they sense their own alienation and estrangement; and yet they go on living in hope, with some degree of concern, and with a kind of natural faith in the worthwhileness of the enterprise. There is alienation, as there is estrangement; there is the lack and failure and absence; there is deviation and frustration. But there is also the ever-present lure towards the better and the capacity to respond, however faintly, to possibilities that promise authentic fulfillment. If the world is not "heaven", neither is it "hell."

In the process perspective, reasons can be given for the state of affairs we have described. The same perspective also enables us to see why it is that nobody can extricate himself or herself, by his or her own efforts, from the situation we have outlined. We are all in this together; hence whatever "salvation" is available must be for all of us. Furthermore, such salvation must be done, not so much by us, as *for* us and in us. In our concluding chapter we shall seek to say something about what God does for us and in us. But now we stress the Christian conviction that "salvation" or human wholeness or rightness, with the possibility of consistently right decisions among relevant openings, is a social and not merely an individual matter. At the same time we stress an aspect of Christian faith that is often forgotten, especially in the Western Christian countries—namely, that the natural order is also somehow included in the salvation of men and women; we belong to that natural order; we are part of it. Hence it is the entire cosmos, including both nature and history, that must be enabled to move forward in the right direction. *How* this has been envisaged in various theologies is not so important as that in many if not in all of them it has been seen to be integral to the picture.

But we must be clear that this is not to be conceived in terms of restoration to some state that supposedly existed prior to failure and diminishment, with their consequent alienation and estrangement. To talk in that fashion would require us once more to take literally the mythology of Genesis; it would also be a denial of the process perspective itself, which insists that the world is an ongoing movement in which there can never be a return to earlier stages or states or situations. Thus the theology that fits such a perspective must by necessity be a theology of *hope*, having to do with what the future may or will be like. The past is never *undone*; its consequences are what they are. What can happen is the setting of that past in the context of a different future. The theology of hope, so often discussed in recent years, cannot properly speak about any return to the past, save insofar as it might pictorially represent the abiding divine intention in such terms. A theology of hope deals with the goals that are ahead and with the ways in which those goals may be reached.

The scriptural term for the goals, taken inclusively, is the King-dom of God; it is a way of stating the realized relationship in which human existence, history, and nature are to share, a relationship between God and humankind and between both of these and everything created. It is the reign of love under cosmic Love, as we have so often said. It is integration and mutuality instead of alienation and estrangement; it is participation in goodness and the fulfillment of self in community with others in and under God. It is belonging to and rejoicing in the natural order, rather than conflict and enmity towards it. It is coopera-tion with Love as Love lures us, and lures everything else, to the greatest possible satisfaction of aim. In other words, the oppo-site of alienation and estrangement is life in love, by hope, and through faith. Or in the language used earlier, it is obedience to the divine purpose or intention of righteousness, goodness, and love.

So far as we are concerned, we can only truly *live* by hope—not in the sense of a wistful and pathetic wish for some-thing good turning up, but in the vital sense of eager expectation that cosmic Love will enable an authentic community to appear. If we have this hope, we can entertain it only by the commitment or engagement of self that is called faith. And here faith really amounts to "life in scorn of consequence", as Kirsopp Lake once said. This means that we ought not simply to set up a contrast between sin and virtue, as if that were the whole story. The real contrast is between defection and distortion, on the one hand, and true fulfillment, on the other; and we shall use that distinction when we come to discuss the traditional list of "car-dinal" or "deadly" sins and their supposed opposites. At the moment, however, we wish to note that in such a context, forgiveness is not the wiping out of a past that has happened; it is the opening to us of new possibilities for self-realization by free and responsible decision, with a future reference and towards ends that are in that future. This opening is based on what we are here and now, for that is where it must be effective. The here and now can only be accepted for what it really is; yet the problem is always what is to be done for and with us as we are, in the situation in which we find ourselves. Under God the here and now can be used in such a way that future enrichment is available and human lives are given the opportunity to decide rightly for better ventures and more satisfactory realizations.

More will be said about this significance as we conclude our study. We now need to consider some of the channels in which alienation and estrangement are concretely manifested. Apart from the effect of the total human situation on each of us, for whom decisions for good become difficult if not impossible, what are the social consequences?

We may speak of these under four headings. (1) There is the breaking of personal relationships and of relationships in smaller groups such as the family or the neighbourhood. (2) There is the conflict between classes or groups of people, such as race against race or labour against management, the "haves" and the "have nots", the rich and the poor, men and women, students and teachers, etc. (3) There is the strife between nations or large sections of the world. And (4) there is the way in which natural resources are used in such a fashion that the beauty of nature is damaged or destroyed and the conservation of nature's riches, for the use of future generations, is disregarded. This is not intended to be an exhaustive list, but it is suggestive of the way in which alienation and estrangement manifest themselves in concrete areas of decision. In what we shall now have to say, we must remember that in each instance we are really talking about such decision-making, whether by this or that person or by the corporate actions of organized or official agencies. Such decisions can hold back, distort, twist, or even prevent the right ongoing of the creative process towards its proper end. This is but another way of putting our contention that every man and woman is part of society and is organic to the natural order, while whatever is done in society and the natural order has its effect upon each.

In each of the suggested categories, it will be convenient to take one specific example that will be representative of others. In speaking of the first, or human personal, area, we shall speak of sexuality. In respect to classes or groups, we shall refer to the racial issue. Strife between nations or sections of the globe will be illustrated by the conflict of East and West. For human disregard of nature and natural resources, our example will be the creation of "dust bowls" in North America. Each will serve to show how the human situation is reflected in decisions that are damaging to the right fulfillment of human potentiality, interfere with the movement towards shared good, and hence deflect the process from its realization of love through righteousness in the area under discussion. Obviously each must be discussed very briefly.

(1) When we consider the question of human sexuality, we need to recognize how it puts before us, in strong relief, the whole issue of human relationships. Sexuality is so deep in us that it is inescapable; it is the basis for our intimate association with others of the race. But it is not always sufficiently understood as being profoundly affected by the situation in which men and women live. Not only do the sexual *mores* or customs, like the institution of marriage or the common contempt for homosexual love, reflect that situation; the prescribed modes of sexual expression and the categorization of other modes as illicit or "unnatural" establish rules that conventional society insists must be followed if the person in that society is to be "accepted" by his or her fellows. The necessity for *some* such guidelines is plain enough; what is not so clear is the way in which those who do not entirely conform keenly feel their alienation and are made to suffer for what often is not their "fault."

In sexual relations, there is always the danger that those who sense their alienation and estrangement will try to compensate by using their sexuality for self-aggrandizement. The sexual partner may become for them simply one who is to be "used", not one with whom a close and enriching contact is shared. A union of lives intended for the better fulfillment of each may be made into an occasion for the gratification of sensual desire without regard for context. There is nothing wrong about sexual desire; it is one of the good things in the creation. But it is taken out of its context of mutuality or love when it becomes a matter of imposing oneself on another for one's own satisfaction rather than for the shared enjoyment of one of life's greatest gifts. The real objection to promiscuity and prostitution or the easy liaison entered upon without responsibility is just at this point. There is a failure to respect personalities in the making. There is a distorting of life's aim and a deviation from the right path to mutual self-fulfillment in which each helps the other along the way.

Despite the conventional notion that such deviation is seen chiefly in homosexual love and its physical expression, in my judgment such love does not at all necessarily fall into that category, provided of course that genuine love *is* in fact present. It is perfectly possible, I believe, for two persons of the same sex to express love, to share love, and to help each other grow in love. Real distortion and deviation, I should claim, come when sexuality (expressed homosexually or heterosexually) reflects a situation where getting is chosen instead of giving, where using is chosen rather than sharing, and where possessing replaces mutuality and the give-and-take that can enrich life.

(2) The racial issue neatly summarizes human alienation and estrangement in classes or large groups of people. Why should there be hatred or contempt for those of another colour? Largely because of fear, it would seem. And fear is itself a striking manifestation of human alienation and the estrangement of person from person. So are the other factors in racial conflict, such as dislike of the colour of a man's skin, rejection of his way of seeing things, and distrust arising from economic considerations like the threat to one's job if those of another race are prepared to work harder or for less wages. All reflect this situation of fear. If people of various races happen to live together in a given community, these problems are likely to be present. We are suspicious of those who differ from us; we are frightened by those whose culture and habits are not our own; we feel imperilled if they are also persons of ability.

Such an attitude is highly dangerous, particularly in a world that is rapidly becoming one great planetary society. Fear prevents the development of a wider family of men that will include all who dwell on the earth; it prevents the establishment of widening understanding and sympathy; it prevents the creation of a just or righteous set of institutions in which every human being is guaranteed the opportunity to become an authentic person. Here is a most obvious example of the situation in which dispute, conflict, and misunderstanding can tear us all to pieces.

Fear is grounded in a desire to be secure in our own position and privileges; and this leads to decisions contrary to the forward thrust in human existence towards a wider sharing of life by person with person, group with group, class with class, and race with race.

(3) The same can be said when we think of the confrontation of East and West, so familiar to us today. It is fear that is the cause of the conflict because fear is an expression of, and accompanies, estrangement from one's fellows and alienation from the creative advance in love. Arguments are produced to justify this fear; like all rationalizations, they contain a modicum of truth. Thus those who live in the West, in countries that are either quasi-capitalistic or are developing into cooperative "welfare states", say that their security is endangered by the socialist economy of the developing lands in the East, especially when with this is associated the communist doctrine that makes an appeal to peoples who have long been greatly impoverished and underprivileged. Revolution or the resort to violence, taken in some of these countries to be the only way to a more just ordering of affairs, is likely to appear an unmitigated evil because it constitutes an overturning of established procedures. On the other hand, people in countries of the East fear the imperialistic challenge, as they think of it, that is expressed today in economic rather than in political form. Furthermore, on both sides the inherited cultural patterns are at stake, along with whatever religious or ethical systems have been associated with these patterns. In a world where nation must deal with nation and where cultural influences are felt despite boundary lines, such a situation is inescapable.

Irresponsible acts on either side provide the material with which this basic fear can work. There are "evil men" in high positions who use such fear for their own purposes. And there can be no doubt that aggression, like the recent Russian suppression of Czechoslovakian moves to "change the face of communism" or the more subtle domination by Americans in the Far East, shows what can happen when fear leads to the suppression of freedom, the imposition of control over thought as well as action, and the eruption of self-righteous anger—and all this quite apart from the appalling suffering that accompanies such ventures. In these ways the human situation as a whole is reflected in concrete acts and with extraordinary clarity. Alienation and estrangement produce disastrous results.

(4) Finally, the failure to respect the natural order and to cooperate so far as possible with natural processes in the development of the resources the world provides can be traced ultimately to a selfish desire to exploit, with no regard for the integrity of nature nor for the consequences that must be endured by future generations. The creation of "dust bowls", our example here, is the direct result of a thoughtless, careless, selfish attitude to nature. It is as if one said. "Let us make a quick profit, getting the most we possibly can, no matter what may happen afterwards." That is an attitude that manifests a disordering of the human situation and expresses in wrong decisions a failure to cooperate with the creative advance towards shared good. It has produced the devastation we see in certain parts of North America, as well as the ruination of nature that seems to accompany all commercial exploitations elsewhere.

In and through these several manifestations of social irresponsibility, self-centred decisions, and thoughtless failure to understand interrelationships in a process that is so remarkably knit or tied together, there is the greater although less obvious alienation and estrangement of people from the movement of Love-in-action in the world. In the last analysis alienation is from God, since it is his aim and lure and goal that are expressed in all creaturely occasions, calling his human children to respond in decisions that promote the authentic good of themselves and others and the world as a whole. And in the last analysis estrangement is from God's loving purpose of more widely shared goodness and from his ceaseless working in nature and history towards the attainment of that goodness. The areas we have been discussing are all secular, to be sure; they do not directly and immediately speak to us of the divine, of cosmic Love at work in the world, of God our Father. But Christian faith discerns that in, through, and under these secular incognitos God's activity is present. Hence to fail in these areas, to distort or misuse opportunities presented by them, and to act as if mutuality, cooperation, and sharing do not really matter, is a refusal to be a co-creator with God, a fellow-worker with him. Thus it is a failure to participate in the deepest drive or thrust in the cosmos.

When people talk about social evils or about the wrongs in the human situation, it is quite likely that they do not often introduce the word "God" into the discussion. This is quite proper, since to do so would be to confuse categories of discourse and could lead to the unfortunate (but prevalent) notion that once God is *named*, nothing further is demanded from us. It is then *God's* job, not ours, to remedy things.

This was brought vividly to my mind when a distinguished bishop complained that God was not mentioned at any place in the charter of the United Nations. Because of this, he said, Christians would find it difficult to be very enthusiastic about what was "only" a secular agency; in any event, he said, it was bound to be a failure since God was not mentioned. I could only wonder at the bishop's theology. Did he assume that the use of the word "God" would be, of itself, a guarantee of stability and an assurance of the value of the organization? Evidently he did. Yet it ought to have been obvious, even to a bishop, that whether or not the word "God" was used, the divine thrust towards human, national, and international harmony was genuinely manifested in the establishment of the U.N. Here there was an effort to set up an international body whose purpose was furthering understanding, good will, and mutual help, averting conflict, and guaranteeing to all people everywhere the freedom that would enable them to live with more dignity, to decide more wisely, and to act more generously. That the United Nations has not always been highly successful in such respects is apparent. But that it is a step in the right direction and in accordance with the divine purpose of righteousness, goodness, and love is equally apparent—even if God is not mentioned by name in its charter.

Finally, some may say that in this and other areas what is really at stake is not goodness and love so much as justice. We have already made some remarks about the relationship between these. But I shall conclude this chapter by saying that the establishment of justice in the earth, in every area of human existence, is the way in which the spirit and attitude of love can best be expressed. If justice means the giving to every person of his or her due, it also means asking every person to act responsibly towards others. That is the mode in which love works when it has to deal with groups of larger or smaller size. Each person must still make his or her own decisions, however. Each must still choose among possibilities relevant to his or her situation. Right decisions will be a reflection of the love which he or she knows and feels, and often enough the working out of that love in concrete practice will involve striving for more justice here and now in the world of human affairs.

In our next chapter we shall consider the specific acts that in traditional theology have been called "sins" — wrong choices with bad consequences for oneself and for others, and against God. We cannot separate anyone from the human situation, but we can distinguish between what that situation is like generally and the specific decisions made by this or that person. So far we have spoken primarily of the situation; now we shall speak of specific decisions.

6
Reinterpreting "Sin" as Acts

For reasons that will appear later, I am not much enamoured of "lists of sin" such as have been devised by moral theologians down the ages. But for our present purposes some such list will be convenient to follow in this chapter where we are looking at the actual concrete decisions each person must make as he or she seeks to move towards what is taken to be the fulfillment of self. In the context of the human situation, with its alienation and estrangement, these decisions are the way in which every person either goes forward towards becoming more and more an *authentic* person, or by wrong choice (and the action that follows upon it) fails to go forward in that direction.

Traditional thinking has almost always placed *pride* at the top of its list of sins. This shows great insight, for (as we shall see) it is in pride, or the arrogation to oneself of prerogatives and privileges that are not proper to self that each of us chiefly expresses present wrongness. After pride, the list usually includes the following: sloth, gluttony, lust, anger, envy, covetousness, dishonesty, stealing. I have extended the list beyond the conventional "seven deadly sins" because I wish to comment on the various sorts of wrong decision we may make; and the conventional grouping of seven "sins" is not sufficiently inclusive for my purpose. Furthermore, I must add what the Middle Ages called "accidia"—listlessness, indifference, or carelessness. After considering these, something must be said about the traditional distinction between "mortal" and "venial" sins, not because that distinction is really valid in the way it has commonly been taken, but because there *is* a difference between fully responsible and conscious election of wrong and the more trivial, perhaps unintended, wrongs we "commit" with little awareness then or later of what we are doing. Finally, we shall

look at the reorientation in thinking about sin or wrongness in
human life found in the words and actions of Jesus—although
what he said and showed was to a considerable extent antici-
pated in the Jewish prophets and indeed by thoughtful and
reflective moralists entirely outside the Jewish-Christian
sphere.

What is the *pride* that sometimes has been called "the root
sin"? I have just spoken of it as the arrogation to self of prerogatives and privileges not properly one's own. That is correct; but
we may fill out the picture by noting that this implies thinking
that each of us is "the monarch of all he surveys", owing final
allegiance to nobody or nothing save himself or herself. Thus it
is the attempt to "go it alone", in the mistaken belief that what *I*
want, as and when *I* want it, is to be sought whatever consequences this may have for others. It is the sort of self-
centredness that overreaches its proper limits; and having put
the self at the centre of things, it then insists upon choosing,
acting, and living as if that self were all that mattered.

We need to be very careful, however, when we talk in this
way. There is a necessary kind of self-centredness that is the
condition of human survival and that is required if personality is
to develop at all. Some have *identified* human wrongness with
the self, in this following what they take to be the teaching of
William Temple who once in an unguarded moment seemed to
urge that sin and self-interest were simply two words for the
same thing. Yet surely there is a *proportionate* concern about
self, physically, mentally and emotionally. Especially in the
years of adolescence and youth, this appears to be an inevitable
and essential part of the process of growing up and of finding
one's identity as this or that particular self. On the other hand,
there is the type of self-centredness that pays no attention to,
acts in disregard of, and takes advantage of, other persons. This
is "individualism" at its worst. The "rugged individualist", to
use a phrase once defended by a president of the United States,
is generally the person who is all out for his or her own interests.
Sometimes this view has been associated with the notion that
such self-interest is bound to lead to the best interests of others,
but surely that is only a convenient alibi and in any event it is

plainly contradicted by much human experience.

The proud person is not in an open give-and-take with his or her fellows. Such a one is likely to use coercion upon them to get his or her own way, or perhaps may exercise that sort of "hidden persuasion", in Vance Packard's words, that is not persuasion at all but a subtle and subliminal way of forcing others to do what the proud person wants them to do. It is hardly necessary to point out the many modern devices for this kind of coercion, some blatant and some concealed.

Now the opposite of pride is commonly and rightly said to be *humility*. That is another word requiring close attention. It may suggest the attitude of Uriah Heep in Dickens's story—a cringing submission, an invitation to others to "walk on me as if I were a doormat." This is often a subtle disguise for pride, which, finding itself unable to get its way by more obvious methods, resorts to a pretended willingness to submit to others while all the time there is a feeling that thus one can achieve one's own desired ends. True humility, a friend once remarked to me, is like having a sense of humour about oneself. It is a recognition of what one is, of one's abilities and disabilities, an honest evaluation of oneself; it recognizes others, too, and sees how we belong together and must accommodate ourselves to that fact. It acts in the same way that it makes decisions—with a grasp of the relativity of all our decisions and their conse-quences in concrete practice, with an honest awareness of our expendability, yet knowing also that we *do* have a role to play and a contribution to make.

In the perspective adopted in these chapters, the choices made in an attitude of presumed superiority, in disregard of others, and without desire to cooperate with the movement of Love in the world are bound to be wrong choices. The person who decides and acts in this manner is one who has mistaken his or her own immediate wishes for the *real* good. No single person can assume that such wishes are the ones that will work out for the realization of the general good of all and for the advance of God's purpose of righteousness, goodness, and love in the world. The humble person understands this; he or she decides, as one must, but decides in a wider context and with consideration for what seems to be best not only for the self but for others, as well as what seems most in accordance with the drive towards more good in the world at large—which means cooperation with the divine activity in creation.

Sloth was the second on our list. Commonly sloth has been defined as laziness in the doing of what we know to be our duty. The slothful person puts off to tomorrow what should be done today; and there is *always* another tomorrow. In the simplest sense, such a person may be called an irresponsible person. He or she would prefer to avoid decisions altogether, since to make then entails at least the intention of fulfilling the demands the decisions impose. Short of that, a slothful man or woman simply delays. Thus in our perspective the slothful person is one who refuses to cooperate in the movement towards good in the world. Somebody else can do that, he or she says. *I* need not do it: why bother? Obviously the opposite of such sloth is an eager *concern* to be "up and doing", to assume responsibility, and to make the decisions required at any given moment and then act upon the decisions that have been made. This need not suggest continual "busy-ness", for often the best decision is *not* to do this or that, or to alter the terms of possibility (as we might put it) so that other opportunities will be available. But the one who consistently puts off decisions and rests content with sliding through life with a minimum of concern and effort fails to take a real part in the creative advance. He or she sponges on others, is a backwater in the ongoing stream of life. The unwillingness to cooperate makes that person an obstacle to his or her fellows and an impediment or hindrance in the general advance toward shared good.

Third in the listing we have followed comes *gluttony*. This is not simply a matter of overeating, as some seem to think! Rather, it is the desire to have too much for oneself, whether this be food or money or anything else. The gluttonous person is not satisfied with a sufficiency for his or her own need or welfare. Such a person always wants more, but wants it for the self alone and would hug that "more", once it has been attained, to the self. It is easy to see, then that gluttony is in fact a manifestation of pride or false self-centredness, just as much as sloth with its wilful refusal, for sheer indifference' sake, to take one's part in the rightful advance of good in the world—because one finds it easier to sit back, like a spectator in a match who refuses to bother with participation in the enterprise. On the other hand, the moderate person, who shows *temperance* in all things—and this is the opposite of gluttony—is considerate of others, sees things more in their right proportion, and attends to the need for an "other-regarding" ordering of life. Such temperance does not imply rejection of the good things in the world. It is a sad mistake to think that because one cannot fairly and decently have more than one's share, one should therefore abstain altogether from whatever good may be available to one. What is meant by moderation or temperance is a right selection and enjoyment of that good, always with an awareness of others and with a recognition that one's own enjoyment should be shared, so far as possible, with those others.

When we come to think of *lust*, next in our listing, we must carefully avoid the error of those who believe that all strong desire, in this instance usually desire of a sexual sort, is by definition wrong. As we have already insisted, there is nothing evil in such desire. Human beings are embodied desires, desires for that which will fulfil them and satisfy their yearning to realize their possibilities, not least in respect to physical relationships with others of the race. Sexuality is a good part of human existence; it is only when it is misdirected that it can become a wrong.

Thus lust is a *good* thing, insofar as it is simply strong desire. It can and does become wrong or sinful when it is expressed entirely apart from the context of love, mutuality, giving-and-receiving, and caring. Lacking that context, it can become destructive of another life and seriously damaging to the self. Here too we see a manifestation of pride, in that one person seeks to impose his or her own will on another, for example by rape, or by simple physical lust without personal concern, giving first place to immediate pleasure without some genuine care for the other person. Like gluttony, lust in the wrong sense is an instance of the inordinate or disordered choosing of self-regarding satisfaction.

The matter of human sexuality deserves a much more extended treatment than is possible in this book. But perhaps enough has already been said to show the central place it has in human existence. Like everything else, however good, sexuality needs control. This need explains why the makers of moral codes have spent so much time finding rules for such control. But they often fail, and their failure is in not recognizing that the control of sexuality, from outside and by *fiat*, is generally ineffectual. It is always possible to discover ways of and reasons for evading these regulations. The only proper control of the sexual drive and desire is from within; that is, by the recognition of love as the basic purpose of the sexual desire and drive, and through the acceptance of control by love as the clue to the right expression of this desire and drive. This tells us that the opposite of lust is *chastity* — but not chastity when it is taken to mean nothing other than abstention from sexual life. John Macmurray has given a better definition of chastity: "emotional sincerity." This sincerity is shown in deep awareness of and concern for others, readiness to respect and honour them, and rejection of the temptation to possession or exploitation of them. A man who in his sexual contacts with his wife makes it evident that he loves her, respects her, and acts in accordance with her desires and feelings, is chaste; on the other hand, a person who has no sexual contacts and yet permits his natural sexuality to show itself in bitterness, malice, suspicion, carelessness, and disregard is *not* chaste. Obviously, for us to talk in this fashion is to suggest a revolution in the common understanding of the word "chastity"; but some of us believe that this revolution is necessary in the light of what we now know about the disastrous human consequences of the attempt at a total suppression of sexual instinct, emotion, and desire.

We now arrive at *anger*. The wrongness in anger is not so much in the violence with which the angry person may happen to behave as in that person's underlying temper and attitude. Anger is loss of self-control and it is lack of consideration for others; it implies quick decisions without attention to all the factors that enter into the situation; it is a thoughtless and careless reaction to what others say and do. In other words, it is still another way in which pride shows itself.

There is such a thing as "righteous indignation", to be sure. Outrage at injustice or at patently wrong actions is necessary; but this is very different from the anger that breaks out violently or quietly expresses itself in hateful attitudes taken in the face of opposition or criticism. The angry person does not "see himself as others see him", nor does he or she take account of views that do not appeal to him or her. One can fail to grasp the truth that even when attack is made upon one, the only genuinely human possibility is our community of persons "in the making" is through giving to each his or her "due." On the other hand, when temper is controlled in the interest of shared good, there can be growth in understanding and a common seeking for values that may be fulfilling for all concerned. Hence the opposite of anger is *charity* of spirit, shown in just such control over tongue and action and in a continual search for modes of sympathetic and understanding relationship with other people.

It is better to "explode" furiously than to repress antagonism and dislike, since repression can mean a festering deep down in human existence that will seriously damage that existence and make impossible any genuine growth. But the kind of "explosion" that exposes others to attack is unhealthy. One need not always "blow up" under provocation. The remedy is to attempt to identify oneself with others, to see oneself in the others' situations, and to sympathize with the problems they face. These things are indeed very difficult, just as for those who are "naturally" (as we say) of a fiery disposition it is hard to avoid the harsh word or the nasty deed. The person who lets anger take possession of him or her is unable to cooperate with good. His or her very fury blinds such a person not only to present possibilities but to the long-range operation of love in the world. Such a person decides too quickly and thoughtlessly; decisions then distort and harm the movement towards good for the self, for others, and in the creative advance as a whole. What is needed above all is to find some "moral equivalent" (in William James's telling phrase) for anger. This can be manifested in indignation against *genuine* injustices and wrongs, and the energy there expended will then not be going against the grain of the ongoing process of good.

We shall consider *envy* and *covetousness* together. The

envious person cannot endure seeing another possess good things that, because they are not one's own, threaten one's sense of security. The covetous person wants for self alone whatever gods others may possess. In each instance we see the desire for shared goods forgotten in the desire to possess for oneself alone. That which is hugged to oneself cannot be shared with one's fellows. Thus both envy and covetousness deny the participation in the common life that is authentic human existence when that humanity is being realized in its right sense. Both are manifestations of the pride that places the narrower self-interest in the centre of life and permits it to govern all decisions. This is why the opposite of envy and covetousness is precisely the *sharing or participation* to which we have so frequently referred.

Dishonesty is the misrepresentation of fact or the refusal to see the fact as it really is. Here we are dealing with a lack of realism in approaching existence. But "truth will always out", in the long run if not in the short one. Dishonesty is self-defeating, for the liar will be "found out" and his or her pretended security will be destroyed. *Truth-seeking and truth-saying* alone make possible authentic life in community; they are the opposites of dishonesty. Even more important, however, is what the New Testament calls "doing the truth"—that is, the sincere and honest *act*, which naturally manifests itself in the honest word. Transparent honesty should characterize each human life, so that each of us may be confident and trusting in our approach one to another. Kant was right in saying that a society that permits lies is one in which such genuine confidence and trust are impossible; in fact, it will be self-destroyed. The untruthful or dishonest man or woman incapacitates himself or herself for cooperation with good and with the movement towards sharing in good, simply because such a person is attempting to fool others and succeeds also in fooling himself or herself. Finally comes the point where he or she cannot see how things go in the world, because acting like that distorts the facts as they really are. Hence the dishonest person eventually loses the clear vision that makes possible such recognition.

Stealing, taking what is not one's own, is a grave refusal of responsibility in the common life. Again it manifests pride, this time pride of possession. Because I do not have what I should like to have, I assert myself in my pride by taking that which is not my own. I think that in this way I can say "This is now *mine*", although in fact I have denied the real truth about the matter and violated the relationship in which alone we can live together in mutual acceptance. Hence the desire to live in just such a relationship of mutual sharing, with the decisions that follow from this desire, will be the opposite of stealing. The wrongness in stealing finds its contradiction in the rightness of participation in the common good.

We have mentioned the medieval classification of *accidia* as a grievous sin. *Accidia* was usually defined as listlessness, indifference, and carelessness. In one way it is close to sloth, for it presupposes a lethargic attitude towards life, leading one to do nothing, to take no stand, to feel bored, and to regard existence as inane and pointless. In the Middle Ages monks and nuns were often said to be ready victims of this fault. They wearied of repeated religious exercises; then they simply carried them on without any genuine interest or enthusiasm. In our own time there are plenty of people in the same case, not so much with respect to religious observances as in their feeling that they "couldn't care less", as the British phrase has it. They find that life has lost its taste and tang. It is hard for them to get along with others, nor can they allow themselves fully to open themselves to the love that eagerly and actively seeks realized good. The contrast here is with a willed and active *participation* in the affairs of life, both in the concrete situations in which we find ourselves and in a purposed relationship with the good that works in those situations.

We have gone through the conventional listing of sins and have discovered that there is a single pattern running through them all. Basically they are manifestations of an unwillingness or incapacity to participate in the basic thrust of life towards future and better realization in love. The one trouble with the traditional list is that it tends to suggest a too abstract view of wrongness; we have sought to replace this, in each instance, with a more concrete and personal portrayal. After all, it is mistaken to *reify* sins, as if they were *things* existing apart from the persons who (as we say) "commit" them. The wrongnesses about which we have been talking are all of them instances of actual decisions made and of concrete acts done, by this or that man or woman. Thus, instead of speaking about "sins", in this abstract fashion, we shall do better to talk about "sinful people"—by which, in our perspective, we mean this or that person who decides in this or that way, for less than the best; and hence who is responsible for projecting or releasing further wrongness into the human situation and thereby impeding or damaging the divine purpose of righteousness, goodness, and love.

Seen in this way, such wrongnesses can meaningfully be regarded as more grave or less grave. This was the old distinction, found in most classical treatments of human sinfulness, between "mortal" and "venial" sin. The former were sins that were so seriously damaging to self and others that they could be said to "kill" (hence they were "mortal") the person who "did" them, insofar as his or her relationship with God was concerned. The latter were the peccadiloes that could hurt or damage but were not serious enough to annihilate the God-human relationship. There is truth in this representation. There are some instances of wrong decision and consequent act that are indeed so frighteningly serious that they can destroy, to all intents and purposes (but *not* finally and completely, as we shall see), the proper relationship of self to others and of self to the thrust of love in the world—to God. There are other instances that are much less serious. But I believe that it is quite impossible to make an abstract listing of "mortal" and "venial" sins and then conveniently place this or that particular wrong in one or the other category. *For it all depends*—it depends on circumstance, on context, and on the concrete act of willing and choosing in this or that given circumstance and context. What matters is the person, not the supposed "gravity" (as the tradition has it) of the sin in some abstract sense. Confessors, counsellors, and spiritual advisers have always known this. Their experience has enabled them to see that in very truth "circumstances alter cases" and that "context largely determines content." Today, when priests, ministers, and counsellors are increasingly obliged to play such a confessional role, it is important to remember this.

In Catholic circles, casuistry has always been a significant part of the confessional relationship. Despite the bad name casuistry has been given, not always undeservedly, it can be and in truth is a respectable discipline—it is the attempt to consider the circumstances and contexts in which wrongdoing occurs, and thus to assist the "penitent" to understand and repent of wrong. It is also the considered and responsible "weighing" of the sin confessed, in order to determine (so far as may be) the degree of personal responsibility involved and the effects the act may have upon others, as well as its seriousness in the God-human relationship. In a way, the casuistic approach to sin resembles one aspect of "situational ethics", in which decisions for or against a possible action must be largely determined by the many various factors of which account has always to be taken.

For our present purpose, what matters however is that the use of casuistry can often lead the counsellor or confessor to see that what in one case might be only a "venial" instance of wrong may in another be "mortal", and vice versa. Thus the distinction is important in itself but the placing of specific sins in one or other of the two categories should not be automatic nor abstract but dependent upon how, what, when, where, and why a particular decision was taken, as well as upon the consequences that followed upon the decision. We can see, therefore, that in any proper study of sins or wrongness in thought, word, and deed, the *big* factor is always the person, his situation, his capacities, and the relevant possibilities that were before him for decision.

At this point it is appropriate to turn to the specific contribution to our understanding of such wrongnesses that has been made by the teaching and activity of our Master Jesus. For here we find precisely this centring of attention on the *person* rather than on the thing done or left undone. As we noted in an earlier chapter, Jesus "interiorized" the whole matter. So far as the gospels provide us with trustworthy evidence of Jesus' attitude, teaching, and activity for others, it is apparent that he was much more interested in the inner spirit of a person than in outward acts and deeds. Furthermore, Jesus was concerned with the tendency or direction of life he discerned in those with whom he was dealing. What he had to say about the "inside of the cup" and about the person who "in his heart" envies or hates or lusts is indicative both of the interiorizing and of the stress on direction. His reading of the spirit of those with whom he had to do was always alert to the fact that all actions, all overt deeds, were manifestations of that inner quality and of that direction of life towards or away from genuine good. His forgiveness was based upon an appraisal of the possibility in each person and upon his or her willingness, deep in interior existence, to take the right path in the future. Others often failed to see this and were less eager to strengthen whatever made for such future good.

Throughout his ministry, Jesus' chief care was to awaken in men their capacity to respond in concern and love. He looked for the development of an understanding relationship with others and an open, frank, and loving response to what they knew of the purposes of God. In Jesus himself men and women saw this at its fullest. Throughout his life what they saw to be his relationship with his heavenly Father determined his relationship to other people. If there is filial obedience to God, there will be loving concern for other men and women. The kind of person whom Jesus commended was like the child who is open-hearted, open-spirited, trustful, and confident, responsive to and spontaneous in the expression of a goodness that is almost unconsciously apprehended and enjoyed. This is made possible in the child because the child knows himself or herself to be loved, to be cared for, to be the recipient of affection from parents. And today we are informed by experts that without such a prior relationship, a child—and the man and woman who grow from childhood into adulthood—will find it difficult if not almost impossible to be that kind of person in respect to other people.

No careful reader of the gospels can fail to notice that Jesus was not interested so much in the sins of those whom he met as in their divinely given potentiality. His attitude towards them was not the negative one of condemnation of wrongdoing; it was a positive encouragement and help in their desire to be truly human—that is to say, truly children of God. In his contacts with others he awakened or nourished that desire. He knew from his own inner experience that the divine Love is seeking always to move through human life and that when this movement is recognized and accepted, even in ways that may seem strange and unconventional, those who recognize and accept it are enabled to make the right decisions and to live in charity with their fellows. If and when this happens in any place or time, there is a glimmering of God's Kingdom which is the reign of Love in the world. There was nothing automatic about it for Jesus, any more than there was anything abstruse or abstract. In concrete instances, in a *this* and a *that*, Jesus expected and awakened the response of faith, which is but a way of saying that he expected and awakened the cooperation of God's children with the purpose God was working out through the creation. There was a place for and a need of human decision; there was responsibility in making that decision. In the end of the day, however, it was for Jesus the Love that is God, and that he called "Father", that came before everything else and that invited the response. God lured and attracted, solicited and drew, people to himself. This came first. But God did not coerce the response, since to do that would have been to deny the love that is his nature and his way of acting with his children. The yes a person might give was necessary; and it had to be the person's *own* yes. The response was inclusive of responsibility, as we might put it. To say yes to God was to accept the responsibility for the decisions one made.

In Jesus' teaching, as well as in his acts, there was no indulging in what Baron Friedrich von Hügel so aptly described as a "spiritual flea-hunt." Jesus was not interested in driving his friends and hearers into a dangerous scrupulosity. That would have defeated his purposes, since it would have meant a concentration of each on his or her own wrongness rather than on the goodness, love, and righteousness of the heavenly Father. Instead of spending time in worry about sin, people were invited to turn to God and open themselves to cooperation with his will; they would recognize soon enough where they had fallen short, gone astray, failed, twisted or distorted their lives. One of the unhappy accompaniments of much conventional talk about sin and sins is precisely in this scrupulosity. Or what is worse, there may be such a continuing introspective analysis of motives and intentions, far beyond the necessary setting of the heart on the right things—"purity of heart", said Kierkegaard, "is to will one thing"—that unhealthy suspicions, both of oneself and of others, are constantly awakened. Jesus clearly did not intend any such introspection. Once a person sets himself or herself to respond to Love, to God our Father, he or she can forget self and act in freedom.

Each of us ought to be aware of motives and intentions, to be sure. But it should be remembered that it is only *God* "unto whom all hearts are open, all desires known, and from whom no secrets are hid." Nobody is able accurately to judge another; neither is anybody able to judge himself or herself as he or she *really* is. To know oneself is indeed good, as Socrates insisted; but no one's self-knowledge is exhaustive and complete. In any event, the more we try to make sure that in every respect our motives and intentions are as they should be, the more likely we are to discover that our purpose in doing this vitiates our effort by making us *wrongly* self-centred. Then we spend time in excusing ourselves, finding ways of "saving ourselves" from ourselves, trying to become good by our own endeavours. Here is the vicious circle to which Luther referred when he said that each of us is *incurvatus in se*, twisted in upon self. As our next chapter will show, only *God* can bring the necessary salvation. Why? Because God is Love, as the Christian faith affirms; he is known to be Love because he has acted and does act *in* love. Moral scrupulosity imperils love, both for oneself and for others. That is why Whitehead was entirely correct in saying that love is always "a little oblivious as to morals."

Now we have been brought again to the point made much earlier in this book: Moral evil and sin are not identical in meaning. Certainly there is a connexion between them; but the connexion does not equal sheer identity. One of the troubles with the conventional lists of sins is that they tend to suggest just such an identity. With all their value, they can become external criteria in terms of which we evaluate what we may be pleased to think of as our moral virtues: "I have not done this; therefore I am virtuous in this respect." So we are likely to think. But this does not take into account the basic and positive question: To what degree, in what way, have I been a personalized agent for the righteousness, goodness, and love that are God's will for his world, the true intention for my life, and the cosmic thrust that in the last resort is God at work in that world? That question cannot be answered simply by finding out that we have *failed* here and there; nor can we claim on our own behalf that because we *have done* this and that we are necessarily the effective instruments for the divine Love that we are being created to serve and express.

We need deliverance from concentration on our own achievements, such as they are, for good or for ill. We need to look at how things are really going in God's world, seeing this with the eyes of faith. We need to give ourselves in response to a Love "that will not let us go." Thus, rather than spending our time thinking about ourselves, we shall lose ourselves in the serving of the good of others and in *the* good, the *summum bonum* or supreme excellence that is God himself. *That* is deliverance from sin; it is salvation from our tragic wrongness into actual rightness. There is no other way; and it is the glory of the reformers, Protestant and Catholic, of the 16th century that in their own way, in an idiom suitable to their own time, they saw this, said this, and called the Christian Church back to the theological affirmation that states it: justification is by grace through faith, issuing in love. This is Catholic truth, as Hans Küng has so well demonstrated in his great book on justification.

Thus we come back to the insistence, so much in accordance with the insight found in existentialism and with the chief stress in process thought, that the truly human life is committed to or engaged in a cause that is inclusive of us but greater than we are, a cause that persuasively and in loving initiative invites and lures response. The fundamental rightness in things, as Whitehead once called it, evokes an answering rightness in us, despite our situation of alienation and estrangement, despite our tendency to choose wrongly. We return to the conviction that we become authentically human when in our inevitable and necessary striving for self-fulfillment we are caught up into and become the agents for the cosmic movement of good in the world. We see that to be a co-creator with God, moving along the routing, or taking the direction, that God purposes for us and that he has given (with its distinctive quality) as an initial aim or vocation for every one of us, is in truth the satisfaction of the desires and drives deep in the total human organism. At the same time, it is the way in which each of us, in company with our fellows, is formed more perfectly, becomes more adequately the personalized agent for the sharing of love, and takes our rightful and intended place as fellow-worker with the divine Love. And we see once again that the process as a whole is towards the greater good, in which each occasion can find its own joy and in which everything contributes—even through pain and suffering, perhaps through tragic deviation and distortion, through wrong itself—to the ultimate fulfillment of the divine intention and the enrichment of the divine life as God receives into himself all the good, true, and lovely achievements of the created order.

In concluding this chapter, two points may be stressed once more because they are of the greatest importance. The first is that most of the areas in which we make our concrete decisions are secular and not specifically religious. There *is* a religious aspect of life—a direct and conscious relationship with God— and it is real and good. But the great majority of the decisions made by men and women, when they choose possibilities that are more or less suited to the fulfilling of potentiality, are in the ordinary day-by-day secular affairs of life. Here God is not vividly and directly before our eyes. He is at work in hidden ways and under one or other incognito. One of the tasks of the Christian is to show that precisely in these areas, with all their apparent secularity, God is indeed present, concerned, and active. The decisions are made, in the last resort, for or against God—in the last resort although *not* always in an obvious way. So the scriptural words are true: "Against thee only have I sinned, and done this evil in thy sight." Perhaps, however, the word "only" is a little misleading, since it may suggest that the sin is not *also* against the creaturely occasions in their secularity. It is in, through, and under the creaturely conditions of a creaturely social process that we sin, just as it is under those same conditions that we serve God.

The other point concerns the futuristic emphasis. What matters most is where we are going, not where we may happen to be at the moment. Our past decisions have gone to make us what we are, restricting or enlarging the range of possibilities open to us at that moment. Our present decisions are largely determinative for us, in our freedom and responsibility, of the path we will take. But what we are to become, what we are in this moment on the way to becoming, what sort of personality we are making of ourselves, are the crucial factors. Nothing remains fixed and unchanging in the world we inhabit and of which we are a part. The question that faces each of us is: Where are you going?

Or, to spell it out more adequately, the real questions are: What decisions are you making that will contribute to your authentic personhood-to-be? To what degree are your decisions, and the actions that follow upon them, assisting in the enrichment of commonalty among people? To what degree are those decisions and their consequences aiding in, or preventing, the movement towards greater good for more people in more ways and at more times—including yourself, too? And finally, to what degree are you contributing to the purpose of God in the world, a purpose that includes you and everything else; and whose end is to be found in a love that is mutual, shared, a giving-and-receiving, a fellowship where each entity participates with every other entity in the most complete society of love, the Kingdom of God?

To answer those questions demands an honesty and a sincerity that takes all there is of a man or woman. We have quoted Kierkegaard's saying that "purity of heart is to will one thing." He might have added that this "one thing" is a love that reflects, because it is grounded in and acts for, the cosmic Love that is called God and that we Christians dare to address as "Our Father."

7

The Overcoming of Human Wrong by Cosmic Love

In the preceding chapter we have indicated the way in which, for Christian faith, God is seen to overcome the wrongness in human decision and action. Our discussion was brief but I hope that the point was made sufficiently clear. In this final chapter I wish to recapitulate the argument of this entire study of sin and its re-interpretation in the light of process thinking, and then spell out in more detail, but of course still inadequately, the Christian response to the situation—or, better phrased, how a Christian understands *God's* response to that situation and to the human condition of alienation and estrangement.

We have urged that the traditional way of dealing with the subject of human sin is so gravely misunderstood today that a new approach is required. The reality to which the traditional concept points is both serious and tragic; it is inescapable for all of us. But the way we look at this wrongness need not be the traditional one. It is perfectly possible to recognize the fact for what it is, while at the same time we seek to put it in the context provided by modern thought, especially (as we have said) the existentialist analysis of human experience and the metaphysical or philosophical conceptuality found in process thought.

In our study we have looked at the human situation in its totality and at the wrong decisions made by men and women in their concrete circumstances. In intention, and I hope in presentation, our purpose has been to emphasize the way in which both our situation and our personal choices are in contradiction to the will of God—a will that intends that righteousness, goodness, and love be the motif of human existence. We have noted

94

that among other defects in the traditional portrayal, as our contemporaries see the matter, is the usual stress on a retrospective rather than a futuristic or prospective picture of human existence, along with a tendency to interpret sin and sins in terms of violations of laws imposed from outside; whereas we should wish to see these same realities of experience as lacks, failures in relationship, and distortions or deviations in the ongoing movement of creative advance.

Certainly some will think that this difference in approach and description necessarily means a denial of everything the traditional view has asserted. To this I can reply only by repeating what has been said earlier. We need to be careful lest we confuse words with facts, conventional ideas with the experience they describe, and traditional concepts with the realities they were devised to indicate. If that has not become sufficiently clear, this study has failed and there is nothing more to be said. All one can hope is that the critic will think again, will ponder carefully what has in fact been said, and will accept the writer's assurance that in his best judgment the situation in which humankind finds itself *is* tragic; that human wilfulness in wrong decision *is* serious; and that our purpose has been to discover how to bring this vividly home to modern men and women. But it would be improper for any author "to protest too much"!

Every faithful Christian will agree that central to the faith, worship, and life of the Christian fellowship is the assurance that God is Love. Even those who prefer to follow the older style, and make aseity or "self-sufficiency of being" the root-attribute of God, will at least accept the fact that in specifically Christian thought such aseity must be qualified by the assertion of God's love, both as his character and as his mode of activity in creation. It will also be agreed that the reason for this central assurance of faith is not found in speculative theory nor abstract argument, but in the response men and women make in commitment of self and in complete trust in the Man Jesus in the fullness and richness of his human existence among us at a particular time and place in history. There, in that Man, a working of God is discerned, such that he is rightly called the incarnation or embodiment of God in genuine human terms. The ancient formula, that Jesus is "God-Man", may not commend itself to us as a useful theological phrase today; but it was one way of asserting exactly this point about Jesus. When Origen, the Greek theologian of Alexandria, first used that expression "God-Man", he was seeking to say that his and our Lord was indeed truly human, but that this same Lord was also the point where true deity has discovered itself to human beings in a supreme and special sense. So too the Council of Chalcedon in A.D. 451 had the same intention when it spoke of Jesus Christ as "of one substance with the Father" and also "of one substance with us"—which is to say, with human existence. We may prefer another phrasing of the matter, but the intention is clear and we are here in living continuity with the theologians of Chalcedon.

The Christian's response in faith to the event of Christ, leading to the conviction that God's very nature and his way of acting is love, must not be thought to suggest that God is active only in that one event and nowhere else. The Christian Church has not wished to say this nor has it ever said it, so far as the main Christian tradition is concerned. Those who have talked in that way have not been representative of this mainstream. For the great tradition, God is everywhere active in the world and in human life; his work is "all of a piece", so that his nature as love is disclosed in various ways throughout the cosmos. Yet in the event of Christ there is a particular and definite disclosure in act, so that what is always true is now *known to be true*. A vivid self-revelation in that one place has provided the clue to all the rest of God's operation in the world. It tells us what he is "up to", what he is doing, in creation. Not only so, but such a vivid and decisive act has its consequences; things are now different from what they were before that act. The dynamic structure of reality now includes this act; the response that has been made to it has augmented the potentiality of a more general human responsiveness to God as he continues to work in and manifest himself through the created order.

But we, in our day, can think of this only against the background of an evolutionary or processive picture of that order. We must say that God operates through a long-continuing movement of creative activity, "making things make themselves" so that they may actualize their fullest potentialities and thus serve the divine purpose. In such a process of creative advance, evil is a present factor with which we must reckon. However, it is not due to God's will nor is it his responsibility, since there are other (although less significant) causative agencies in creation. It is those agencies that through creaturely decision, of differing intensity and with varying degrees of conscious awareness (minimal in the physical realm, greater at higher levels, very considerable with human beings), bring about deviation from the ongoing of the creative movement towards its intended goal of a goodness shared as widely as possible. In the concrete human situation, and for this or that particular person, there is both the possibility of wrong decisions and the actuality of such decisions, with disastrous consequences for the advance. God purposes that "all things work together to a good end"; wrong choices interfere with that working and prevent its full realization. They *count*; and, alas, they count for ill and not for good.

The greater part of the wrongness both in the human situation and in human decisions is manifested in the ordinary affairs of secular existence. There is not an obvious, conscious, and intentional violation of the divine will in most of these instances. Nonetheless, the fact is that such wrongs *are* violations of the divine will, whose characteristic is the expression (in concrete acts) of righteousness, goodness, and love. This is because God is both the chief creative agent, the chief causative agent, and the chief recipient of what goes on in the world. He is present in and working through all created occasions. To harm one's neighbour is, in the last resort, to hurt God, to go against his will, and to impede his plan. The First Epistle of John is quite plain about this: It is impossible to claim to love God when one does *not* love one's brother. The secret of the world's existence, the meaning partially hidden and partially revealed in its mystery, is nothing other than the divine love in action. Anything and everything that is against that love is wrong: it is either evil or sinful.

We have spoken of the redemptive or saving activity of

God, but full and proper consideration of this activity would require writing another book. It is not my purpose in this concluding chapter to embark on any such enterprise, but it is essential that we conclude our discussion with some further remarks on how God has acted and does act to overcome the wrong in the world. Elsewhere I have discussed the matter more fully (e.g., *Theology and Reality*, Seabury Press, 1955, pp. 109 ff.; and *God in Process*, S.C.M. Press, 1967, *passim*). For our present interest, let us simply begin by stating what is implicit in Christian faith: Because God is himself Love and Lover, he cannot permit lovelessness, human wrongness, or any other kind of evil to persist uncontrolled and unchecked.

Love is diffusive of itself, concerned with others, and it can never contemplate a state of affairs in which that which violates love shall continue; it must seek to do something abut the matter or else it is not genuinely love at all. To say this is different from saying, with much traditional theology, that God's *justice* has been offended by such wrongness and that he must remedy the matter so that this justice may be established beyond question and may be *seen* as thus established. I cannot think that this view is sufficiently Christian. It is not so much God's justice that has been violated by wrong as it is his love. To put things in that way changes the whole picture very radically. No longer are we thinking of a judge who administers the law nor of a monarch who wishes nothing but obedience from his subjects. We are now thinking of a loving Father who desires only the best good for his children; who, when he sees that those children do not act lovingly one with another or towards him, wishes to bring them to himself and to their fellows in a realized attitude of love and in the actions that would express it; and who goes out searching for ways in which they can be brought to that realization and expression, utterly responsive to the love that is of God and that is God. To that end he will do all in his power.

All in his power, yes. But God's power in respect to his human children is not coercion, even if he must exert force here and there, more particularly at other levels of creation, to keep the ongoing process moving in the right direction and within the limits of order. With men and women God's "power is chiefly in showing mercy", as an old prayer puts it; his real exercise of power is in his self-giving, his readiness to identify himself with others, his suffering of anguish and his undergoing of pain, if by such means he may secure the free, willing, and responsible "amen" of those whom he so passionately loves. Throughout the creative process God works this way; among men and women he has never failed to move towards them and to work in them with such love.

In the course of human history there have been those who have grasped this and responded to it. They have lived at many different times and in many different places. Perhaps they have not had a vivid realization that the working of love they have known and to which they have responded is nothing other than the reality of God himself. Nonetheless they have been aware of that which came to them to win them to love, to vanquish their lovelessness, to conquer their alienation, to overcome their estrangement from one another, and to make available to them genuine authenticity of life. In Jesus Christ, however, there has been an intensification or focusing of this love-in-action—let us now say this *Love*-in-action, for we are speaking of the personalized reality of God as he communicates himself to his human children. Through the whole event of Christ—including the preparation for his appearing, the facts of his temporal life, and the consequences that have followed upon it—God was active in a singularly compelling way. The compulsion was the compulsion of love, not of force. For to put it almost blasphemously, God knew perfectly well and God knows perfectly well that the only way in which lovelessness can be overcome is by transforming it into love. And that demands nothing like pressure, coercion, or an overriding of freedom; it requires, on the contrary, that the Lover, namely God, shall be "first in loving", as St. Augustine so strikingly phrased it. By being first in loving, he can win from those who are loved a returning love that will give them wholeness and rightness and thereby redeem them from the lovelessness that is the exact opposite of such wholeness and rightness.

"Having loved his own that were in the world, he loved them unto the end. . . ." So John's gospel speaks of Jesus. What does he intend by the words he uses—" the end"? It could mean simply the conclusion of his life among men. But I think that the Greek words, *eis telos,* shows that the Evangelist means some-things more than that. He is speaking of Jesus' having loved "his own" *to* death and *in* death and *through* death and to the fullest possible degree. The proof of this extended meaning may be seen when we recall that for St. John the Cross is Jesus' "glorifi-cation" and hence constitutes his real victory. "I, if I be lifted up, will draw all men unto me"—all men, and all things too—the entire created world. Easter Day with its message of resur-rection or risen life is not the reversal of Good Friday with its placarding of Jesus' death before our eyes. It is the validation or vindication of that which Jesus did on Good Friday; it is God's way of declaring that death "can have no dominion" over love like that, because it is God's own self, his very being, his nature, which in Jesus' human loving was actively at work and had engaged itself in a victorious struggle with what is wrong in creaturely existence. Only in *that* sense can we speak of rever-sal. For on Calvary there is the disclosure in act of the im-mortal, unchangeable, persistently seeking Love that is God himself—and *that* "cannot be holden of death."

This action of God in Christ awakens the response of faith, which in turn awakens love and inspires hope. But it does more than this. For if each event in the creative process makes a difference to every other event, having consequences that reach out in every direction—a point we have shown to be integral to the process conceptuality—then *this* event of Jesus' giving him-self in such utter love makes a very great difference indeed. The ongoing movement in the world now includes the fact of Christ; it includes this inescapably and with no possibility of loss. This constitutes what an older theology rightly spoke about when it noted the *objective* aspect of the Cross. It means that things are now different. But there is the *subjective* aspect too. For we now can make our response to God in terms of that which has taken place, whether or not we do this in full awareness of what we are doing. God is not only vividly revealed as Love; he has been decisively active as Love and this activity has had its result in the structural patterning of the dynamic advance in creation.

The Calvinistic school of theology used to speak of "common grace" in the world. This phrase denoted a working of God in the creation sufficient to prevent things from getting altogether out of hand and to provide the inspiration, the strengthening, and the natural human decencies that make our human existence a possibility. Surely there *is* this "common grace" and we shall do well to recognize its presence and acknowledge its effectiveness. But there is also the specific "grace of our Lord Jesus Christ," through which we are brought into the "fellowship of the Holy Spirit" and assured of "the love of God." In Jesus' life and death and certified by his rising-again, the divine Love is poured out in abundant measure, like the Holy Spirit who (says the Fourth Evangelist) was present in such abundance in Jesus. The grace of Christ is shared with those who in commitment and trust respond to what in Christopher Smart's fine phrase God has "determined, dared, and done" in that place, at that time, by that means. The consequence of this sharing of the Spirit is life "in Christ", as St. Paul says over and over again. Those who are Jesus' people live in him and he dwells in them. So to live makes possible the right decisions and the right actions that follow upon them. The human situation is altered for good, since now the "bundle of life" in which we are to be knit together is seen as the life of perfect love, manifested through and active in that Man and in the association with him that the same apostle could describe only by referring to it as membership in "the Body of Christ."

There is no instantaneous alteration of the world of humankind. The "old Adam" is not killed outright; he must be "mortified" in the long process of living in Christ "the new Adam." Human existence in God's intention is there, in Christ; and there is a continuing "sanctification" or making Christlike of those who have been given "the right to become sons of God". More and more of concrete existence is to be included as continuing response is made to God's purpose of righteousness, goodness, and love, until "Christ is formed" in his brothers and sisters. William Law spoke aptly of "the process of Christ"; for him this was what Christian life was all about. It is a fine phrase, since it stresses both growth and Christ *in that growth*. It has to do with the "knowledge and love" of God and of our human companions, which works in the disciple to replace wrongness in thought, work, and deed, by a sharing in the cosmic Love that is God himself.

What has just been said is merely a restatement of the doctrine of justification by grace through faith, resulting in sanctification in love. As the doctrine has often been presented, it seems to make little or no sense to our contemporaries, who do not naturally think in the traditional terms. Yet it is indeed, as Martin Luther once rightly said, "the article of a standing or falling Church". It is utterly central to Christian existence. But it is not a discovery of Luther, to be sure; it is essential Christian conviction, based on abiding Christian experience. St. Paul knew it and taught it; so have all the great thinkers in the Christian tradition, both Catholic and Reformed, even if from time to time its meaning has been slighted and its centrality unrecognized. And all faithful Christian discipleship has been based upon it.

The traditional idiom is not very useful in our own day. Nonetheless, the doctrine is an account of God's way of overcoming what traditionally we have called sin and sins. Whatever words we may wish to use, this is how God puts us on the right path, gives us the right direction to follow, and lures us to himself. So it is God's way of bringing his human children, in all their wrongness, into a right relationship with himself as the great cosmic Lover. Through the divine Love, shared in human solidarity, human alienation and estrangement are overcome and God's children become whole. "Thanks be to God, who hath given us the victory through our Lord Jesus Christ."